Marketing Powerhouse Series

How to Write a Proposal That's Accepted Every Time

The Practitioner's Guide to Great Proposals

Second Edition

Alan Weiss, Ph.D.

KENNEDY INFORMATION

PETERBOROUGH, NEW HAMPSHIRE

ISBN 1-932079-11-4

About the Author

Alan Weiss is an internationally-known consultant, speaker, and author. His firm, Summit Consulting Group, Inc. has successfully competed against the largest consulting firms in the world to work with prestigious clients such as Merck, Hewlett-Packard, Chase, Avon, Mercedes-Benz, GE and hundreds of others like them around the globe. He is the author of 21 books appearing in six languages, including the revolutionary consulting best-seller *Million Dollar Consulting: The Professional's Guide to Growing A Practice,* with its emphasis on value-based projects and the abandonment of per diem fees.

Dr. Weiss welcomes comments from readers and can be reached at Alan@summitconsulting.com or http://www.summitconsulting.com. The interested reader will find hundreds of additional, complementary articles and resources available at the home page for downloading on this and related subjects.

The author wishes to thank Maria, Danielle, Jason, L.T., and Phoebe for their assistance with this book.

Contents

Why We Created a Book About Proposals

Over my 26 years of consulting, the two most frequently asked questions of me by other consultants have been:

• How do I write an effective proposal?

• How can I establish value-based fees?

Consequently, my colleagues at Kennedy Information and I decided that these would be two "must" books in our three-book series of "Marketing Powerhouse Series." This is the second edition of one of the most wildly popular books I've ever written.

In order to write an effective proposal, you must understand that the written document itself is only one step in the process. It is a culmination, not a beginning, a summation, not an exploration. The *process* of proposing a project to a client is important to grasp and understand conceptually before anything is put on paper.

That's why we feel this book is so unique.

There are books available with proposal templates, contracts, legal provisions, and formulaic "boiler plate." This book, while providing plenty of examples and models, details the specifics of how to acquire the information that creates winning proposals *in collaboration with the buyer.* And therein is the key to proposal acceptance: collaboration with and agreement by the client prior to anything being committed to paper.

We've also dealt with the land mines: committees, gatekeepers, focus on fee (rather than value), RFPs (requests for proposals), delays, legal eagles, and many more of the inevitable booby traps and mazes that occur in every organization. But whether you deal with the public sector or the private, large companies or small, charitable or for-profit, domestic or global, manufacturing or service, we've provided a process that is applicable to *your* customer.

We can't guarantee that every proposal you submit will be accepted, even if you follow all of our advice. But we can guarantee that you'll submit fewer meaningless proposals, improve your hit ratio, and have the opportunity to gain higher fees if you do take this book seriously.

Do we really know what we're talking about? Well, we did get you to buy the book, didn't we . . .

—Alan Weiss, Ph.D., CMC
East Greenwich, RI
April, 2003

Action Items

Action Items

Action Items

Chapter One

What is a Proposal?

Let's get the easy stuff out of the way. A proposal is simply an offer of ideas or actions extended to another party for consideration and agreement.

If I suggest to you that we go to the local theater tonight to catch the Laurel and Hardy Film Festival, I'm making a proposal. It's an idea that might or might not capture your fancy, and which you may accept, alter, or reject. (My wife invariably rejects Laurel and Hardy, my proposal utterly lacking value for her.) If you suggest to a prospect that you can alleviate the prospect's client attrition problems through a six-month, $350,000 intervention, that, too, is a proposal.

It's helpful to understand that proposals are not inanimate documents which occur at some point in a business deal. Those documents, when they exist, are merely tangible summations of the ideas being agreed upon. In the business environment, proposals are actually based on *conceptual agreement* between you and a prospective client about *what* is to be accomplished, *how* it will happen, *when* it will occur, *where* it will occur, *who* is accountable for its occurring, and, most importantly, *the degree to which you will confidently know it has occurred.*

The term "conceptual agreement" is one I coined in the early 90s as it applies to consulting. It refers to commitment between buyer and consultant on the objectives (results) for a particular project, the metrics (measures of success), and the value to the client organization (improvement or worth). *If you have not established conceptual agreement, you have no business writing a proposal, much less submitting one.*

> Written proposals are formalized arrangements of ideas and actions for consideration and acceptance by the prospective client.

When people say, "We sealed it with a handshake," what they mean is that they gained conceptual agreement on those factors and demonstrated their intent to move ahead. If documents followed later, they were merely a formality to enable others to understand what's intended, satisfy legal requirements, and/or stipulate payment terms.

In the consulting profession, proposals should be *summations and not explorations.* That is, a written proposal should merely summarize the conceptual agreements previously established, and provide the opportunity to review them in writing, select possible options for implementation, verify the payment terms, and formally consummate the relationship. Written proposals are static. They do some things well, but can't do some other things at all.

Proposals can and should do the following:

- Stipulate the outcomes of the project

- Describe how progress will be measured

- Establish accountabilities

- Set the intended start and stop dates

- Provide methodologies to be employed

- Explain options available to the client

- Convey the value of the project

- Detail the terms and conditions of payment of fees and reimbursements

- Serve as an ongoing template for the project

- Establish boundaries to avoid "scope creep"[1]

- Protect both consultant and client

- Offer reasonable guarantees and assurances

Proposals cannot and/or should not do the following:

- Sell the interventions being recommended

- Create the relationship

---

[1] "Scope creep" is that phenomenon where a project oozes outside of its original intent, bloblike, because the client keeps asking for additional services and the consultant keeps providing them because there are no clear boundaries to the project. The result is insolvency for the consultant.

Action Items

- Serve as a commodity against which other proposals are compared

- Provide the legitimacy and/or credentials of your firm and approaches

- Validate the proposed intervention

- Make a sale to a buyer you have not met

- Serve as a negotiating position

- Allow for unilateral changes during the project

- Protect one party at the expense of the other

- Position approaches so vaguely as to be unmeasurable and unenforceable

- Describe the backgrounds of the consultants

- Incorporate legal jargon and boilerplate

I know this last point is highly controversial with many of you and certainly every lawyer, but bear with me. You'll see as we proceed that the last place in the world you want your proposal to visit is the client's legal department, yet placing boilerplate in the text absolutely guarantees that odious journey.

As in comedy, timing is everything

One consultant I know makes an overly huge point that "proposal" denotes "marriage" and that the term "agreement" is superior. Others like to use "contract" or "working relationship." No matter what you use, clients are smart, and know what proposals are. The key is that the consultants also be smart, and realize what their proposals can and can't—or shouldn't—do.

The very worst tactic to use with a proposal is to create it too early in the cycle shown in Figure 1-1.[2] The object of following up on a lead should be to achieve a personal meeting. The object of the first contact should be to hold those meetings and discussions necessary to reach the true buyer.[3] Those meetings and discussions should be focused on gaining conceptual agreement, as described above, on the project outcomes, measures, and accountabilities.

[2] We'll discuss RFPs (requests for proposals) and other situations when this cycle is not possible later in this book. However, the sequence presented is usually the case in most private sector work.

[3] The buyer is that person who can actually cause a check to be signed, payable to you, without any other approvals. I call this person the "economic buyer," as opposed to feasibility buyers, who may like you, but can't pay you.

In the sales sequence, the role of the proposal might look like this:

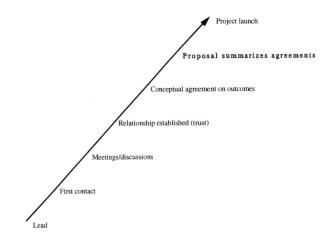

Fig. 1-1: The proposal's place in the project life cycle.

For example, in discussions with the buyer you may arrive at the following:

Objectives:

- Reduce customer attrition from the present level of 25% per year

- Implement procedures to prevent such a level from recurring

- Initiate reacquisition, where possible, of last year's lost customers

Measures:

- Next year's attrition is lower than the past year's

- All sales managers follow up on each account monthly

- Reacquisition of five clients who left in the last 18 months

Timing:

- Begin with new fiscal year (November 1)

- Complete outside intervention by March 1

- See attrition rate drop in second and third quarter

- Realize two former client reacquisitions by third quarter

- Sales managers have visited all existing accounts by fourth quarter

3

Action Items

Methodology:

- Interviews with current and former customers
- Interviews with best salespeople (lowest attrition)
- Focus groups with field sales force
- Focus groups with operational support people
- Visits to current client sites
- Training sessions and procedural review with all relevant personnel

Joint Accountabilities:

- Client will provide access to all key personnel
- Client will schedule customer access
- Client will provide names of former customers to contact
- Client will provide all classroom and administrative/logistical support
- Consultant will provide all personnel for interviews, focus groups, training
- Consultant will sign nondisclosure agreements as required
- Consultant will provide timely reports of progress, scheduled and on demand
- Consultant will create all support materials and provide copyright to client

Note several things. First, these details of agreement are gained through discussion, and probably over several meetings (although not necessarily if you reach conceptual agreement rapidly). Second, they can only be gained with the true buyer, that person who is responsible for outcomes and whose budget is at stake. I call this person the "economic buyer." Third, *there is seldom the need to do an extensive needs analysis to gather this information.* There will always be further information required—that's what the focus groups and interviews are for—but for the purposes of acquiring information for a good proposal, *that information is usually in the possession of the buyer.* Later chapters in this book will provide help in asking the right questions to extract that information.

The purpose of the conceptual agreement stage, then, is to enable you to create a proposal which summarizes those key points already on the table and agreed upon. At no time did the conceptual agreement stage attempt to delineate fees. All prospects are interested in fees, and most consultants are too eager to provide them. *If you've been*

successful in achieving conceptual agreement on project outcomes and support features prior to the proposal, the fees will be a nonissue. That's right: If you present a proposal which summarizes what is already agreed upon, the resultant fees will receive far less scrutiny *since the focus has been moved from cost to value.*

> Extensive needs analyses delay proposals and are seldom necessary. The true buyer will almost always have all the information required for a comprehensive proposal. The consultant has to know what to ask.

The point of gathering the requisite information and agreement to complete a proposal in my process is that you focus exclusively on *value* and never on fee. If you're discussing fee prior to the submission of a proposal, you have lost control of the discussion. My observation and mentoring leads me to believe that at least 90% of consultants allow the prospect to discuss fees far too early in the process.

Thus, one of the primary purposes of a proposal is to move the prospect's attention to the value—output—side of the equation, and away from the investment—input—side of the equation. This is why the relationship building and conceptual agreement stages are so integral to a successful proposal.

Every single client or customer I've ever met wants to reduce costs. But every one of them also wants to maximize value. It's up to you where you allow the focus to be placed. A premature proposal will focus on cost; a properly-positioned proposal will focus on value.

In Figure 1-2 you can see the difference in perspective. Prospects always have a very clear view of costs (or want to acquire that view). They have a budget. Or they have to take money from something else. (Most consulting needs are not funded in advance.) And, while they know they want relief from some pain or help with some improvement, there is always the question of how much they might realistically achieve and how they'll know they've achieved it.

That's why a clear conceptual understanding of the outcomes is important in order to establish the significant benefits to be derived, and the proposal serves as a guarantor of a fixed cost to achieve those desirable benefits.

Action Items

How a prospect might view a project:

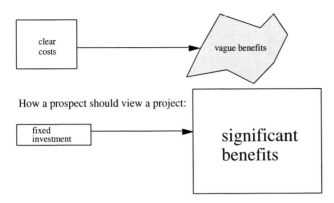

How a prospect should view a project:

Fig. 1-2: Positioning investment vs. benefit prior to the proposal.

Only three things can happen, and two of them are bad

Woody Hayes, when coaching football at Ohio State University, was asked why his teams seldom threw passes. "When you put the ball in the air, only three things can happen (completion, incompletion, interception), and two of them are bad. Why do that?" was his reasoning.

As we stated above, a proposal only has three outcomes:

1. Rejection: The proposal is not acceptable and the prospect is not inclined to continue discussions or amend it.

2. Alteration: The proposal has mixed benefits and value to the prospect, but the prospect is willing to negotiate, counter-propose, or seek some changes. Those changes *almost always will involve added value for the same fee, lower fees for existing value, or both.* Consequently, alterations are not usually good for the consultant.[4]

3. Acceptance: The prospect accepts the proposal, often choosing from among options provided by the consultant within the context of the proposal.

The lesson from Woody Hayes is: Don't throw the proposal up there unless you're reasonably assured of outcome #3. There is no retreat from outcomes #1 and #2 to regain #3, hence, the need to carefully gain conceptual agreement prior to submitting anything in writing.

[4] Many consultants will agree to practically anything in order to get the work, which is pure lunacy. When working on a project for the American Institute of Architects, I asked some of their members how they could continue to take on projects at a loss. "We make it up on volume," they replied, only half-jokingly. Over the past decade, architects' earnings have actually declined in real dollars, despite a boom economy. It's better to have no business than bad business.

The proposal, therefore, is really the capture of a sequence of events which happen to be formalized in a written document at a certain point in time. To do that prior to those events being successfully completed is to invite outcomes #1 and #2.

Summary of Chapter 1:

- Proposals are based on conceptual agreement of project outcomes.

- Only a true buyer can be party to the conceptual agreement for proposal acceptance.

- Timing is situational, based on how long it takes to move from initial contact, through relationship-building to conceptual agreement.

- Proposals don't "sell"; they confirm.

- Proposals are summations, not explorations.

- Successful proposals require diligent preparatory work.

- The prospect must be focused on value, not cost.

We'll turn to the required preparation in the next chapter. Historically, I've "hit" on about 80% of the proposals I've submitted. But I submit many fewer than most consultants. As in most of consulting, less is more.

Quick Start: If nothing else, remember that you must secure conceptual agreement on value before discussing fees. You control this, not the prospect.

Self-Assessment Questions:

1. What percentage of the time do you submit proposals to clients prior to establishing clear conceptual agreement?

2. What percentage of your proposals are accepted?

3. What percentage of accepted proposals are unchanged by the client (especially the fee structure)?

4. How often do you focus on value rather than cost or task?

5. What do you do to ensure that you are meeting with the economic buyer?

Action Items

Interlude: Value-Based Proposals (and this very book)

The proposal approach which I present in this book is based in turn on my concept of value-based fees. That is, fees should be based on the value derived by the client and the consultant's contribution to that value, and not on the traditional and highly delimiting "time and materials" formulas used by lawyers, accountants, architects, and the like.

The book you're reading is an example of such value-based pricing. It is among my very best-selling books (I have published 21 as of this revised edition) despite it's higher-than-average price. I have a tough time keeping it in stock.

At various times, people will contact me and assume there's been an error. Typically, someone says, "There's a typo in your catalog, because your proposal book is listed at $149 when it must really be $14.90."

When I tell them that $149 is accurate, I get a bewildered stare when I'm present, or an abrupt silence on the phone. "Surely," I'm told, "you can't be serious."

One woman told me that she'd never buy a book which costs almost a dollar a page. "Do you buy books based on weight and volume?" I asked, "or based on value and contribution to your life?" I theorized that, if the former, *War and Peace* must have been a great bargain for her.

She insisted that a book should only cost a few cents a page, and I knew we had nothing left to discuss because she didn't "get it" and this book could never help her in any case. If price is based on value, why should a book be exempt from that equation?

The test, of course, is in the marketplace, and I have several books selling at this price point, and other products even above it. I've been told constantly by readers that the concepts in this book have added tens of thousands of dollars to their annual income, sometimes quite quickly since many people purchase the book in anticipation of a proposal that is imminent. Thus, the logical question: If a book improves your business by tens of thousands of dollars annually, is $149 a worthwhile investment, and is the result a decent ROI? (Even if the book increased your income by $2000, isn't 13.5 to 1 a fine return?!)

Consultants buying books needed a slight reeducation, perhaps, to appreciate that dynamic, but a great many quickly accepted the premise. We have to engage in the same educational process with our buyers—demonstrate significant potential value, using our relationship-building to partner with them in determining it, and create our fees in accordance with that value. By dint of reading this book, you've made that value decision (assuming you haven't stolen or borrowed it!) and therefore *are probably rather committed to embracing the concepts herein and putting them to work for your benefit.*

Since I'm "preaching to the choir," I want to capitalize on that dynamic. That's exactly what we should be doing with our buyers as consultants. Once they embrace the notion that the project is valuable and your fee commensurate with that value, they have a vested interest in ensuring that the project proceed. You don't want this book to fail you because you want to have made a good investment, and the client wants the project to succeed on that same premise.

Whenever you encounter a buyer who seemed previously committed but is now strangely silent, apathetic, or even antagonistic, you can bet that there was neither a strong, visceral buy-in to the organizational value nor the personal value to be derived. (See another of this book's "interludes" to learn about personal objectives underlying corporate objectives.)

As you can see in the graphic below, fee tracks value from the outset. That is, the more the perceived value, the higher the fee that people are willing to pay.

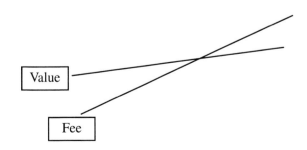

Action Items

But what's not commonly appreciated is that *there is a point at which the lines cross.* Once a premise, brand, approach, name, or other alluring appeal is sufficiently established, then the higher the fee attached the more commensurate worth and quality are associated with it.

No one seeks the cheapest heart surgeon, or bargain shops for second-hand fire extinguishers. Nor do we expect to pay a cut-rate price for a top-of-the-line Mercedes, a Bulgari watch, or Manalo Blahnik shoes. In fact, we'd doubt the authenticity if the price were markedly lower than what we normally associate with that level of quality.

In summary, the higher the fee, once you're established and known, the more impressive you are and the more value that accrues to you. Buyers have egos, and don't want to be known for buying a cut-rate consultant any more than a heart patient wants that bargain-basement surgeon. This book and its price are proof of that.

If this weren't the case, you wouldn't be reading these words right now.

Action Items

Chapter Two

Five Steps to Ensure Success

Proposals are not accepted or rejected on the basis of a document that the buyer reads. They are almost always accepted or rejected based on the *prior* discussions, agreements, and relationships that were formed leading up to the submission of the proposal. So before we actually tackle the construction of a proposal (in Chapter Three) we're going to focus on the preparatory work that will tend to guarantee its warm reception.

Disregard this advance preparation at your own risk.

In this chapter we'll examine the following techniques that are essential to master *prior* to creating a proposal for a prospect:

Five Techniques to Master Prior to Creating a Proposal:

1. Determining who the economic buyer is and how to reach that person

2. Developing a relationship with the economic buyer

3. Establishing outcome-based business objectives

4. Establishing measures of success

5. Assessing value

Step 1: Determining who the economic buyer is

There are a variety of people who appear as "buyers" in organizations, no matter what the organization's size or focus. The trouble is that consultants often confuse them as being equal in the decision making process. Submitting a great proposal to a non-buyer or non-decision maker is like placing racing tires on a '68 Volkswagen. Not only will the car not go any faster, it probably won't move at all.

The typical array of "buyers" a consultant encounters may be characterized as:

- *The Economic Buyer:* This is the person who can cause a check to be signed. He or she needs no other approval, has the budget, and has the volition. In larger organizations there are hundreds of economic buyers. This is not hierarchically-related, unless you're dealing with a small company, where the owner, CEO, or another top person makes all purchasing decisions. The key is budget approval, not rank or title.

- *The Feasibility Buyer:* This is typically the screener who's been asked to find candidates for a given job. It can be a secretary, a vice president, or a committee. Nevertheless, these people have the job of presenting likely candidates to the real economic buyer. Feasibility buyers are notoriously conservative, because they are concerned about their reputations in terms of whom they place in front of the real buyer. One critical point for all consultants: Committees are invariably feasibility buyers. Committees virtually never have budget and never decide; they recommend to someone (either a member of the committee or someone else). Don't waste time submitting proposals to committees.

- *The Implementation Buyer:* This is typically a meeting planner or event coordinator, whose job is to ensure that everyone is focused on a central theme or purpose. They are running a meeting, conference, or workshop. They may be easy to reach, but they cannot buy, only recommend to someone who actually owns the budget. In the speaking profession—and this includes those consultants who also deliver training, facilitation, keynotes, etc.—it's common to get locked up with meeting planners whose job it is to *preserve* money, and not to invest it. ("I'm sorry, we'd love to hire you but we just don't have the budget.")

- *The "Shadow" Buyer:* This is anyone from a prospect organization who agrees to meet with you. Consultants often determine that it's easier to "get in the door" with anyone who will open it, on the assumption they can then roam the halls and find someone with money to spend. The exact opposite is the case. If you get tangled up with people who can't say "yes" but can say "no," then they will ultimately tell you "no" regardless of how many times you've met, or (shudder) bought them lunch, or talked on the phone. In fact, economic buyers are not impressed with consultants who hang around lower-level people.

Action Items

Low level people are invariably paid to conserve budget, while higher level people are inevitably paid to get results. The motivations of different hierarchical positions are fairly constant:

Lower levels: Motivated by security and safety. Simply want to retain a job and collect a pay check.

Middle levels: Motivated by the great American dream of opportunity, egalitarianism, and upward mobility. Hence, they are very conservative, since promotion in large organization means not making mistakes (much more than risking setback in order to achieve great victory). They don't want to rock the boat.

Higher levels: Motivated by power, and will readily take prudent risk, find additional resources, and develop support in order to advance his or her goals (and, hence, accrue more power).

In summary: Only economic buyers have the three ingredients needed to purchase your services (and, therefore, seriously consider a proposal):

1. Budget

2. Accountability (and volition) for business results

3. Willingness to invest the first to achieve the second

They may have titles like vice president of sales, or director of marketing, or assistant treasurer, or manager of field education. Titles don't matter, particularly in larger organizations.

How do you tell if you're dealing with an economic buyer?

Very few business cards say, "Jane Jones, Economic Buyer." So, barring the obvious (e.g., you're talking to the CEO), how do you determine who the economic buyer is?

I suggest that you work a series of questions into your discussions as early in the relationship as possible. You needn't ask these as if they are a checklist, and you can apply your appropriate level of tact (a real "driver" might say, "Who's budget will support this?" while a more mild-mannered type might say, "Who might sponsor this initiative?").

(Note: See the "101 Questions" which I've developed as a guide for you at the end of this book.)

Ten questions to determine the economic buyer:

- Whose budget will support this initiative?

- Whose operation is most affected by the outcomes?

- Who should set the specific objectives for this project?

- Who is the most important sponsor?

- Who has the most at stake in terms of investment and credibility?

- Who determined that you should be moving in this direction?

- Whose support is vital to success?

- Who will people look to in order to understand whether this is "real"?

- Whom do you turn to for approval on options?

- Who, at the end of the day, will make the final decision?

Add your own questions, but you get the idea. You seldom have to ask more than a few of them. Once the same name keeps being mentioned, you know who your economic buyer is.

> Proposals that are sent to anyone other than an economic buyer are the equivalent of leaving on the landing lights for Amelia Earhart: a nice gesture, but ultimately futile.

It's essential, early in the process of attempting to establish relationships, that you quickly and accurately identify the economic buyer for any particular project. The failure to do so not only delays you, but it might relegate you to a level in the company which will taint your credibility with the real economic buyer. A typical example: Line executives seldom place great credibility in their internal human resources function (usually for good reason) and that taint will extend to consultants recommended by that function.

One final fail-safe point: If the person to whom you've been talking constantly states that he or she is the one making the decision, and the questions above all end with that person's name, *then ask one final question:* "So, if you and I reach agreement on how to tackle this project, we can shake hands and begin, is that right?" If the person hesitates, equivocates, stutters, mumbles, or stares blankly back at you, keep searching.

Like Diogenes, you still haven't found the honest man.

Action Items

How do you escape the gatekeepers?

Those people who can't buy from you but who see their job as protecting the buyers are often called "gatekeepers." Every one of us in any consulting discipline has encountered these gatekeepers. These are people who have either been expressly instructed to ensure that the actual buyer isn't disturbed by actual sellers, or they are self-appointed guardians of the higher elevations. In either case, they can't say "yes" but they can say "no," with the inevitable result that they usually say the latter.

Our job isn't to be liked, it's to obtain business which commensurately delivers value to our client. If I sound as if I'm being harsh about not wasting time with gatekeepers, it's because I am.

How do we get by such entrenched defensive positions without being killed in the attempt? There are three options that I've seen work well:

1. **Enlightenment.** Through the force of your moral and rational argument, influence the gatekeeper to open the gate that leads to the economic buyer.

2. **Guile.** By flexibility and tenacity, work through other openings in the defenses.

3. **Force.** Overrun the defender using clout, volume, or sheer bravado.

Examples:

The **enlightenment** approach means that you appeal to the rational self-interest of the gatekeeper. You have to make him or her look good, and provide strong indications that introducing you to the buyer (or at least not watching while you enter) provides virtually no risk and the possibility of significant credit.

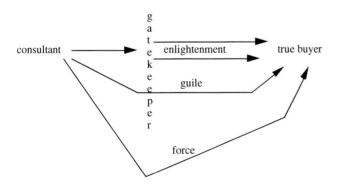

Fig. 2-1: Three methods to get past gatekeepers.

I was pursuing the CEO of a $500 million organization whom I had briefly met at a trade conference. He had indicated a need for an organizational audit, and invited me to "contact his people." The gatekeepers here were those "people": a committee of mid-level managers who had been empowered to evaluate all consultant approaches and decide on a "final five" to reach the high ground. I quickly learned through phone conversations with the members that they had never done this before, were using criteria better suited to evaluate workshops and training programs, and were obviously trying to mask their ignorance in assessing consultant capabilities. When my turn came to meet with the committee, I provided them with a set of criteria to measure consultant capabilities for their situation (i.e., Fortune 500 experience, line management experience, specific management audit references, etc.), told them they were probably using some version of these parameters (which, naturally, they were not), and proceeded to demonstrate my worth, using my own criteria! Needless to say, I passed admirably. I also provided a set of guarantees my firm provided (i.e., interviewing each of them individually, should we make it to the next round) to convince them that their objectives would be considered even after I was admitted to the buyer's sanctuary.

I became their preferred choice and won the contract. I had learned this path the hard way, having had gatekeepers refuse me at a prior prospect when I gave a "canned" presentation and was upstaged by some far better, customized approaches by rivals.

Guile is a productive tactic, because it prevents the gatekeeper from becoming angry with you while at the same time neutralizing the position. While dealing with a particularly intransigent human resources director at a large division of a client with whom I consulted in other divisions, I recognized that a director of marketing had been with the division which was my client. I sent him a note explaining that I was trying to see the vice president of sales of his current division, dropped some mutually recognized names from the "old days," and sent him some sales articles which I thought might be of interest. Then I told him when I would "be in town" seeing the gatekeeper again.

We went out to lunch and he agreed to provide an introduction to the sales executive I was pursuing. The three of us met for lunch on a future trip, and six months later I had a project. I kept up my relationship with the gatekeeper, studiously thanking him for his help and patience. There's no need to make an enemy in this process. He understood the coincidence of my contact's position, and didn't feel offended.

Action Items

Finally, **force** is required much more often than we'd like to think. But we can't afford to waste precious time and energy on people who can't say yes, and many consultants spend too much time nurturing these pointless relationships.

There's an ethical imperative to meet the buyer

My definition of force is simple: I'm going past the gatekeeper, hopefully peaceably, and with a good reason, but I'm going in any case, even if it means bad blood and sniper fire. I typically say in such instances that my approach to formulating proposals is based upon discussions with that person whose investment is at stake, who will be evaluated on the results, and who will be accountable for evaluating the outcomes (the buyer). I explain that professionally *and ethically*, I can't submit a proposal or respond to an RFP without such a relationship, and that none of my current clients ever expected anything less. About half the time, those arguments will win the day, albeit grudgingly.

The other half of the time I simply contact the buyer by phone, FedEx, or e-mail and explain that I'd love to be considered for the project but unfortunately I can't become involved unless we have a brief meeting to discuss objectives, measurement, and mutual accountabilities (and, of course, to build the relationship between the two of us). If I'm told that other people don't require such meetings, I respond by pointing out that such criteria are what make me unique and of singular value. If I'm told that the gatekeeper really can't be circumvented, then I explain that the buyer is denying him- or herself the application of their own experience and perspective to make a selection for such an important assignment.

In one case, in a huge high-tech firm, I was responsible for getting a gatekeeper transferred when the buyer found out that the image being created and the arbitrary filtering out of consulting alternatives was not serving the organization well.

There are some fine people doing their best to protect superiors from incessant sales calls. There are also some weak people who see their sole value and power base in playing the role of junkyard dog. As consultants, we can't submit an effective proposal to improve the client condition unless we meet with the person who can set objectives, decide on measurement, commit collaborative resources, and sign our check. If we settle for anything less, we're kidding ourselves and deserve to be sitting in someone's waiting room reading magazines.

Whether we use enlightenment, guile, or force, it's up to us to reach the buyer before we're trapped in the eternal entryway. People who can't say "yes" but can say "no" will always, ultimately, say the latter, no matter what kind of relationship you develop with them.

Starvation is as deadly as a bullet, and usually a lot more painful.

Case history: Successive gatekeepers, or light at the end of the tunnel

I was called by a human resource vice president to ask if I'd be interested in meeting with his colleagues to discuss a project on merging cultures after an acquisition. I agreed, and met with him and two peers in New York. I quickly ascertained that they were feasibility buyers, who were regretful that their boss, the senior vice president, had to leave unexpectedly prior to the meeting.

I focused on developing a relationship with them, seeking only the small "close" of a meeting with their boss. Indeed, I was their favored alternative, and the next meeting occurred with them and their boss. However, I learned during that meeting that he, too, was a feasibility buyer, in that final economic approval had to come from the CEO, personally. Consequently, I developed my relationship with him and offered to return as soon as the CEO was available.

The next week I met with the senior vice president and CEO, who rubber-stamped our prior discussions. I had to attend three meetings—with no thought of remuneration for my time, although expenses were paid—develop relationships with four people, and continue to be available for questions just to meet the economic buyer. But that was all right, because my path was constantly upward and each "gatekeeper" saw their rational self-interest in helping me to the next level. This is of far higher quality than either guile or force.

Finally, by the time the CEO said "yes," there was not one scintilla of fee resistance in the building. Virtually any fee I set would have been accepted.

Action Items

Step 2: Developing a relationship with the economic buyer

Once you've reached the economic buyer, a proposal is still a long way off. The immediate need is to develop a relationship. Let me define the kind of relationship that will ultimately produce the ability to gain conceptual agreement:

The relationship with the buyer should be a peer-level, mutually-trusting interaction, in which both parties are comfortable being candid, and sincerely believe that the other will always act in their mutual best interest.

Trust is the honest-to-goodness, deep-seated belief that the other person has your best interests in mind. Hence, I will listen to critique if I trust you, but will probably doubt praise and accolade if I don't trust you.

In other words, the buyer has to believe that you will be honest about your capabilities and sincere in your willingness to provide real value. You have to believe that the buyer is describing the problem honestly, and will provide the support you require—as partners—throughout the relationship.

The first stage in this kind of relationship-building is **active listening**, or what the psychologists call "reflective listening." Consultants are too prone to besiege the buyer with their strengths, features, background, and SAT scores in the subconscious panic that they will not be seeing that person again any time soon. Of course, if they act that way, they won't be.

Rather than talk, consultants have to listen, but listen in such a way that they are actively engaged in the conversation, nonetheless. This means paraphrasing, summarizing, and repeating what the buyer has said. The process might look like this:

Buyer: I'm concerned about our decreasing growth in market share, because this is a highly competitive business and if we're not taking share, then someone is taking it from us. There are very few new clients or unknown existing ones. We know where they live, and so do our competitors. It's increasingly a commodity proposition.

Consultant: In other words, your market share is growing, but not at the rate you'd like?

Buyer: That's correct. We're at the stage where we've forced out the smaller players or driven them to niches we don't care to pursue. We have to be more aggressive with our major competitors, and of course they're taking the same position toward us. We have to be aggressive, but also protect our existing client base from erosion due to their efforts.

Consultant: So you need a good offense and a good defense?

Buyer: Exactly.

In this interchange, which actually happened to me, there is no need to tell the buyer about similar situations you've worked on elsewhere, add your latest reading on the issue, or ask questions that disrupt the conversation flow.

The second step in relationship building is to **provide value early**.

I was once asked by a consultant to review a form he was going to pass out to a group of executives at Michelin Tires for whom he was asked to give an overview of his consulting approaches. The economic buyer was in the room with all of his direct reports. The form basically stated that the ideas described during the presentation were the sole intellectual property of the consultant, and that the people in the room agreed not to use them unless the consultant was actually hired by the company.

"What do you think?" asked Jack.

"I think that you should just walk in and tell them that you don't trust them and get it over with."

Case Study: How to listen. REALLY listen.

I was sent to a $400 million division of a Fortune 25 company. The parent told me that the division's newly appointed president had already been through four consultants, but nonetheless needed help structuring his organization. They arranged the meeting, but told me that I was on my own. It was his budget and his decision.

After saying "hello," the CEO talked for almost an hour, barely pausing for breath. He told me of the division's past, its present, and its future. He told me of his plans, his hopes, his anxieties. Every two minutes I'd merely utter "really," or "so, in other words . . ." or "I see."

Finally, he ran out of gas. He looked me dead in the eye and told me that I was the first consultant who had ever sat in his office who really understood his business. He hired me on the spot, and the deal led to five annual retainers in excess of $100,000 each. Looking back, I probably earned about $25,000 per word I said during that one-sided but powerful conversation.

Action Items

"Don't be flippant."

"I'm not. This form has the exact same effect."

Trust has to be both felt and demonstrated.

After you've practiced active listening, **do not** attempt to solve the prospect's problems. After all, nothing is that simplistic in business, and it's presumptuous to assume that you can suggest resolutions after 45 minutes that the client couldn't come up with in 45 days of trying. However, it is highly appropriate and quite powerful to begin to provide valuable *insights.*

Those insights might include at this point:

- Similar situations you've seen and/or read about.

- Your personal experiences with similar issues.

- Books or articles which bear on the problem.

- A contact or reference who has experienced the problem.

- A concise description of the issues you heard that were of most import.

- Questions to help clarify the problem.

- Some reactions to what the client seems to be doing *well.*

> The key to providing value early is to have the client begin thinking, "If I'm getting this much from an informal meeting, what would I get if I hired this person?"

Relationship-building is based on these two simple premises: listen carefully, summarizing or paraphrasing what you've heard; and provide value early, whether with ideas, reading, referrals, clarifications, or any other devices available. You'll know the relationship is solid when the buyer has shared personal insights and intimate details of the situation, your questions are answered promptly and candidly, and the buyer begins to ask your opinion and to use you as a sounding board.

These are the magic words from a buyer who is happy with the relationship, after you've suggested an idea or approach: "You know, we've never looked at it quite that way before."

Step 3: How to establish outcome-based business objectives

The most essential ingredient for any successful consulting intervention—and, consequently, for any proposal leading to such an intervention—is agreement on business-based outcomes. There are two elements here: The objectives must impact the business of the buyer (e.g., ROI, ROA, ROE, market share, attrition, productivity, image/repute, safety, etc.), and they must be outputs, not inputs. Consulting studies, seminars, focus groups, training, interviews, reengineering teams, and so forth are simply means to various ends. Those ends are what constitute the buyer's needs, not the methodology to reach them.

An objective is a desired business result. It is never a "deliverable," task, or input.

Examples of input vs. output:

Input	*Output*
• Run sales training sessions	• Improve sales closing rates
• Conduct focus groups on morale	• Improve communication laterally
• Interview former customers	• Reduce attrition rate
• Audit recruitment process evaluation	• Increase retention of new hires
• Redesign performance	• Provide higher quality, more frequent performance feedback
• Review expense procedures	• Decrease travel costs
• Improve senior officer teamwork	• Enable decision making at proper levels
• Study technology needs of service personnel	• Improve service response time

The early death knell for many proposals is that they revolve around methodology, prompting the client to ask if there are less expensive and less intrusive interventions, and prompting feasibility buyers to point out that "we've already tried that." By focusing on outcome-based objectives, the proposal prompts the buyer to focus on key business (and emotional) needs that he or she fervently needs corrected or improved. The methodology becomes far less important, because the results take center stage.

Here are some questions to ask (depending on level and nature of the project) to develop outcome-based objectives once the relationship has reached the point of comfort and trust to do so.

Action Items

Questions to ask to develop outcome-based business objectives:

- How would conditions improve as a result of this project?

- Ideally, what would you like to accomplish?

- What would be the difference in the organization if we were successful?

- How would the customer be better served?

- How would your boss recognize the improvement?

- How would employees notice the difference?

- What precise aspects are most troubling to you? (What keeps you up at night?)

- If you had to set priorities now, what three things must be accomplished?

- What is the impact you seek on return on investment/ equity/sales/assets?

- What is the impact you seek on shareholder value?

- What is the market share/profitability/productivity improvement expected?

- How will you be evaluated in terms of the results of this project?

Note that none of the questions is activity-driven (e.g., "Would a focus group be acceptable culturally?"), some relate to strategic issues and other to tactical issues, some relate to higher level economic buyers and some to lower level, and none is mutually exclusive. There's nothing wrong with having such questions written and available in your daily diary or business portfolio, so that you can refer to them as a checklist when the time is right. I've found that the responses to them are of far higher quality when they are asked interactively by the consultant, rather than provided as an "assignment" to the buyer for completion.

In many cases, the buyer responds, "You know, I've never really thought about it that way," in which case you're also cementing the relationship.

Outcome-based objectives allow you to frame the project, avoid "scope creep" later on, determine whether the expectations are reasonable, determine whether you have the competency to meet them, and enable you to proceed to measures of progress against those objectives.

Step 4: How to establish measures of success

There are those who say, "If you can't measure it, it doesn't exist and it's not important." I don't know about that, but I do know that if you can't measure progress toward meeting the client's objectives, then your proposal has no foundation.

Some of my clients call these "metrics." Others call them "measurement devices." The terminology doesn't matter. In essence, you're asking the client a derivation of Robert Mager's famous dictum: "How would you know it if you fell over it?" Objectives are useless if you can't tell whether or not they've been achieved. Knowing that the train is heading for New York is not very helpful if you don't know whether it arrives today, tomorrow, or in two weeks.

A measure is an indicator of progress or accomplishment of an objective based on observed behavior and/or empirical evidence.

In rather interesting studies taken at major theme parks, it's been determined that people waiting in gigantic lines for popular attractions are much more prone to tolerate the wait and remain cheerful if two circumstances prevail: First, there are periodic signs informing people how long they have to wait having reached that point in the line; in this manner, people feel informed and can manage their own expectations. Second, the line has to move frequently, no matter how slowly, *and no matter if the movement comes from an artificially longer distance to create the sense of progress.* In other words, small victories and a sense of movement are important.

After gaining agreement with the prospect on the outcomes, it's time to ask how progress toward them should be measured. There are only three responses to that question:

1. The client says that there are existing measurement devices that can be used.

2. The client asks that you suggest some measurement devices.

3. The client says that no one has thought about that.

The second and third responses are very productive, because they allow the consultant to provide that added value once again by suggesting some alternatives to measure results. That very act creates a continuing diagnostic partnership between consultant and buyer. Also, the consultant is in a position to create measuring yardsticks that he or she know are comfortable and appropriate, given the objectives already established.

Action Items

The first response also provides opportunity. The consultant should review those existing metrics to ensure that they will effectively measure progress toward the particular objectives that have been established. For example, a weekly sales report system might not actually provide measures of customer satisfaction, but only customer contact. It's useful to separate the qualitative from the quantitative.

Questions to ask to establish measures of success:

- How will you know we've accomplished this objective?

- Who will be accountable for determining progress, and how will they do so?

- What information would we need from customers, and in what form?

- What information would we need from vendors, and in what form?

- What information would we need from employees, and in what form?

- How will your boss know we've accomplished this objective?

- How will the environment/culture/structure be improved?

- What will be the impact on ROI/ROE/ROA/ROS?

- How will we determine attrition/retention/morale improvement/safety?

- How frequently do we need to assess progress, and how?

- What is acceptable improvement, and ideal improvement?

- How would you be able to prove it to others?

Note that some measures are strictly objective and quantifiable: improvement in profit, increase in retention, decrease in attrition. But others will be subjective and more qualitative: improved public image, better cross-functional collaboration, improved morale. The important thing isn't to nail down every objective to some definable metric, *but rather to agree on how it will be measured and who will do the measuring.*

I've had executives tell me that their measure of improved team work is that they are called far less often to play "referee" with subordinates who refuse to compromise, and they have to make far fewer decisions at their level that should have been resolved among direct reports. I'll al-

ways accept that measure, because it will be accurate, highly personal, and easy to discuss in terms of observed behavior. In fact, the more the objectives involve interpersonal actions (cooperation, responsiveness, supportiveness, etc.), the more you'll want to used observed behavior and environmental evidence in the measures.

Now that you've established objectives and measures of success, there is one final aspect of conceptual agreement required prior to actually creating your proposal. And it may be the most crucial of all, because it is the only way to determine what the proper fee structure is likely to be.

Step 5: How to determine the value of the project

In my experience, most consultants drastically undercharge and over-deliver. That's because they don't have clearly circumscribed objectives (so they deliver until the client is sated even after the project objectives are actually met) and they are locked into primitive per diem billing systems (and there are only so many hours in a day, and so much that can be billed per hour).

The value of the project is the client's acknowledgment of how much better off the organization is, quantitatively and/ or qualitatively, as a result of the objectives being met.

In establishing fees that are proper investments for the buyer and fair profit for the consultant, you must start *at the other end—the output end.* You must establish the value of the project *in the perception of the buyer who will write the check* prior to determining what the proper fee levels are. Unhappiness (and rejected proposals) about fees are seldom the result of proper or improper fit against the objectives to be accomplished. They are usually the result of cognitive dissonance of the buyer—the fee does not seem to represent a logical investment in terms of the ultimate value, because the value is seen in the input, methodologies, and deliverables, rather than in the business outcomes. Fortunately and unfortunately, that is a dynamic which the consultant can and must control.

Inevitably, the inability to set appropriate fees is the result of vague or absent value acknowledged by the buyer.

Project value is based on two major issues: First, what is the value of the business outcomes (as expressed in the objectives) to the buyer? Second, what is the unique value that the consultant brings to the partnership?

The first question should be resolved during the conceptual agreement stage by asking a series of questions.

Action Items

Questions to establish value with the buyer:

- What if you did nothing? What would be the impact?
- What if this project failed?
- What does this mean to you, personally?
- What is the difference for the organization/customers/employees?
- How will this affect performance?
- How will this affect image/morale/safety/repute?
- What would be the effect on productivity/profitability/market share?
- What is this now costing you annually?
- What is the impact on ROI/ROA/ROE/ROS?

> If you want to make a lot of money and create a practice that is worth more than just the name on the door, you must base fees on value. Per diem billing is crude, inappropriate and, ultimately, unfair to the client.

The second set of questions you ask of yourself.

Questions to establish your personal contribution to value:

- Why me? Can any consultant do this, or do I have special attributes?
- Why now? Is the timing particularly urgent or sensitive?
- Why in this manner? Is there some aspect of the methodologies or relationships that are key at the moment?
- What's unique about our relationship? Does the buyer place special trust in me?
- What's my unique value-added? To what extent can I "guarantee" success and exceed the buyer's expectations?

By combining the buyer's assessment of project value with your assessment of your personal value, you're in a position to formulate options and fee ranges in your written proposal.

Case Study: Using value to differentiate yourself

I was one of a half-dozen consultants being interviewed by the economic buyer and her team for a major redesign effort at a large bank. At my interview, the executive began telling me about the company, why the redesign was deemed necessary, appropriate and inappropriate interventions, and so forth.

When she asked if I had any questions, I said, "What's the value to you of doing this? You've told me the impetus, the pros and cons, and the overall game plan. But what will it mean if it's successful?"

She thought a few moments, and then encouraged her staff to contribute. I wrote down comments such as:

- We'll attract and retain key customers at less expense.
- Our public image will improve dramatically.
- Third parties will refer to us more readily.
- Failure work will be eliminated.
- Executives can get back to strategy from "hands-on" management.

I told them that in view of those very legitimate expectations, that some of their premises about implementation were right on target, but some were not. I explained that I wanted to work "backwards" with them, to arrive at implementation steps that would ensure the value they desired. They enthusiastically participated.

I was told later that I was really selected for the assignment as soon as I refocused them on value-based outcomes. Once again, the fee was inconsequential compared to the outcomes I had them concentrating on.

The trusting agreement about objectives, measures, and values is what I've called "conceptual agreement." Simple as that, and as powerful as that.

Quick Start: Find the economic buyer quickly, at any cost. Nothing else speeds up your sales process as much, or undermines it as greatly if you don't do it.

Action Items

Summary of Chapter 2:

- Only the economic buyer can truly accept a proposal. You should deal with gatekeepers through self-interest, guile, or force. Whatever you do, don't waste time at that level.

- Once you've ascertained that you've met the economic buyer and you've established a trusting relationship, there are merely three aspects of the project that require conceptual agreement *prior to your proposal:*

  1. What are the business outcomes desired (because that is the basis of the value to the client)?[1]

  2. What are the metrics that will be applied (because those are the devices which verify that the value has been delivered)?

  3. What is the value of the outcomes (because that is how to base your options and fee structure)?

- Determine your unique value-added.

- There are specific questions to ask (cited above and again in the appendices) to complete any of these five "success" steps if you're not sure of the circumstances or what to do next.

- This preparatory work will be the main determinant of whether or not your proposal is accepted.

Self-Assessment Questions:

1. How often do you systematically verify that you're dealing with the economic buyer?

2. Do you have plans to successfully deal with gatekeepers in the short-term?

3. Do you have the business vocabulary and contemporary knowledge to be seen as a credible partner for an economic buyer?

4. Can you recognize and/or create outcome-based business objectives for the potential project?

5. Do you ensure that you establish the value of the successful completion of the project in collaboration with the buyer?

---

[1] And this applies equally well to nonprofits, government agencies, education, and any other market. All organizational buyers have outcomes that they need to accomplish.

Action Items

Chapter Three

How to Structure a Written Proposal

> Some of you have turned immediately to this chapter. Welcome. If you read some phrases such as "conceptual agreement" or "metrics" that don't make sense to you, then you're probably best served by reviewing the first two chapters.

Over 90% of the proposals I've seen are too long because they have so much extraneous information. The primary cause is that those documents are being used as sales tools—explorations—rather than confirmation of conceptual agreement—summations.

In my experience, almost any project that reaches this point in the process described in the previous chapter can be summarized in about 2½ pages. You might require 2 or 4, but that's about it.

There is no evidence that longer proposals are more effective and, since I've assisted many firms in dramatically reducing the length of proposals with a commensurate increase in "hit rate," I could make a case that less is more. And consider the productivity increase inherent in spending less than half the time to produce an equally (or more) effective proposal as before.

Proposals longer than that fall victim to one or more of these land mines:

Information overload: The consultant is attempting to impress the client with data, and/or gain credibility through volume. At times, the information is simply a substitute for the fact that there are no tangible objectives that have been developed on which one can hang one's project "hat."

Verbal runoff: Less is always more when you're trying to obtain a buyer's quick approval. Some consultants are so impressed with their own expertise, rather than with the buyer's needs, that they believe they must discourse on everything they've learned since their freshman year in Psychology 101.

Credibility desperation: When the relationship and ensuing trust required for the project's acceptance have not been previously gained, consultants wrongly believe that extended résumés, biographies, testimonial letters, and assorted honorifics will win the day in the proposal. In fact, no buyer cares what you've previously accomplished; the buyer only cares about his or her immediate business needs.

Legal weasel: The boilerplate about "being held harmless" and "interest will be added if unpaid . . ." and "the party of the other part" usually means that there have been too many lawyers involved (the critical minimum of "too many" being just one). My rule of thumb is that if you can't do business with a handshake, then you haven't established a relationship. Some client organizations will provide their own standard contracts for signature in additional to your proposal. My feeling is that this important summary document, intended to finalize the sale, is no place to create concerns that need to be interpreted by conservative third parties (*viz.:* the legal department).[1]

Preoccupation with size: Alas, many consultants seem to believe that size does count. Hence, they bulk up their proposals with graphs, reference works, diagrams, articles, project maps, and any other tchochkes that can be stuffed between the covers. If you're concerned about the size of your firm or staff (or, more precisely, lack of same) deal with it on your own time or with your therapist. The client requires quality not quantity, and excess quantity will *always* subordinate quality.

---

[1] If you aren't comfortable unless you create a legal contract, then see *A Legal Road Map for Consultants* by attorney Judy Gedge (Oasis Press, 1998. Grants Pass, OR). This is a concise booklet that will provide the specifics on contract requirements for both your proposals and your practice. Also see *The Complete Guide to Consulting Contracts* by Herman Holtz (Upstart/Dearborn Publishing, Chicago: 1995).

Action Items

The nine components
of a good proposal

Here is what constitutes a proposal that avoids the land mines above, focuses on prior conceptual agreement, provides an orderly and logical flow for the buyer (a series of small "yeses"), and allows for the options that can dramatically increase fee ranges. We'll discuss each of the areas in detail below.[2]

1. Situation appraisal

2. Objectives

3. Measures of success

4. Expression of value

5. Methodologies and options

6. Timing

7. Joint accountabilities

8. Terms and conditions

9. Acceptance

It will be useful to use a specific, consistent example as we walk through the proposal elements. Here is a brief scenario that we'll use to formulate each step.

Scenario: We have been meeting with a series of people at Hewlett-Packard in Palo Alto, California. At the third meeting we were introduced to the vice president for organizational effectiveness, whom we ascertained was the economic buyer. In two meetings with her we've learned that HP has been through a long period of growth that resulted in resources being added to the organization with immediacy and urgency, but not with any comprehensive plan. The Compaq acquisition has added a new urgency to the situation.

Now, post-acquisition, during a slower and more cost-conscious period, the organization has become concerned about overstaffing, turnover, misallocation of talent, and a lack of alignment between some jobs and corporate goals. Line management has become sensitive to all opportunities to reduce cost and, rather than use draconian reductions in head count, the buyer wants to create an organized and systematic approach to recruitment, retention, and development. She also believes that staffing reductions will ensue from this more rational approach to resource allocation.

[2] There are sample proposals in the appendix and on the CD with content included from actual client engagements.

We are now in a position to offer a proposal. We'll create one using this scenario and the steps cited above.

1. Situation appraisal

Proposals should start with a *brief* description of the current situation. This serves two immediate purposes:

1. The situation appraisal lays the groundwork for everything that follows, since it describes the problem to be solved or the situation to be improved.

2. The situation appraisal is a restatement of the conceptual agreement gained earlier, *so the proposal can begin on an acknowledged point of agreement.* This is an important psychological advantage.

The situation appraisal *is not* a description of the organization or a book report on its activities. It is a concise, pithy synopsis of why you and the client are considering the partnership being proposed.

> Situation appraisals enable you to begin on a point of agreement, not contention or even uncertainty, which is important for the series of small closes that should ensue.

Here are examples of two situation appraisals that could be written for the same proposal.

Situation appraisal example #1:

Hewlett-Packard is a world-class provider of computer hardware, software, and test instruments which is considered to be a desirable place to work by both recent graduates and professionals considering career changes. The company has an extensive field recruitment effort reporting to the human resources department. This function is responsible for placing about 90% of all candidates for posted jobs, whether the source is internal or external. Last year, approximately 1,400 people were recruited, hired, and/or placed through this avenue.

The company is looking for ways to reduce duplication of human resource and internal client recruiting efforts, and to attempt to measure for the first time the retention rate of candidates secured through various means to determine if there are patterns related to candidate source and job satisfaction and performance. The vice president of hu-

Action Items

man resources is searching for a firm to analyze present efforts, recommend adjustments, and help in the implementation of a new, coordinated, and measurable process.

Situation appraisal example #2:

The company's recruiting and job placement efforts are currently deemed by senior management to be uncoordinated, overly expensive compared to other firms, and not correlated with success or lack of success on the job. They have not been adjusted to reflect the acquisition. There is certainty that the system can be streamlined and improved, both in terms of return on investment and candidate attraction, retention, and ultimate performance. No such study or analysis has been conducted in anyone's memory.

When the organization is able to assign accountability for identification of job needs, candidates, and proper alignment, it will be able to avoid "reinventing the wheel" each time it seeks to fill a position. In addition, positions will no longer be automatically filled without an analysis of job need, proper credentials, experience, and reason for the incumbent's departure being performed first. This improvement in hiring and placement has implications for cost control and performance for every operation in the company.

Review the two examples, and write some of the distinctions of the second one, compared to the first, in the space below:

_____

_____

_____

_____

_____

_____

_____

_____

Here are my candidates for the key distinctions of example #2:

- It did not provide a company history to people who clearly know their company's position, but rather described the issues.

- It stated business outcomes (e.g., increased performance, cost control) and not inputs (reduction of duplication with human resources, attempts to measure).

- Value was introduced, as were specific instances of improvement (analysis of jobs and incumbent departure prior to automatically filling the position).

- Strong opinion was offered with phrases that will linger ("reinventing the wheel," "no such study ever conducted").

- The view was comprehensive (implications for every operation) and not staff-related (human resource duplication with line partners).

- It provided a concise description of a key business problem that should gain both the attention and agreement of any parties reading it, whether they were part of the original discussion or not.

- No solutions were implied (duplication of effort) that might suggest the answers are obvious and don't require much assistance for resolution.

Note that the situation appraisal can be easily accommodated in two paragraphs. Most business issues can be, so long as you confine yourself to a brief description of the major problem or improvement articulated by the buyer in prior conversations. It's always helpful to use any key phrases, company jargon, or colorful descriptions the buyer might favor ("We reinvent the wheel every hour around here") as well as to add your own observations *that were previously discussed with and agreed to by the buyer.*

The situation appraisal should be the first thing that the reader sees, should occupy the top third to top half of the first page, and should result in the readers figuratively or literally nodding their heads in agreement as they move on to the objectives for the project.

2. Objectives

As stated in the prior chapter, objectives should be business outcomes. They are not interventions, not tasks, not consultant intentions, and not anything that hasn't already been discussed and agreed upon during the conceptual agreement phase. And they should pass the "So what?" test. If any proposed objective can be stalled and require re-explanation after being challenged with "So what?" it simply isn't strong enough.

Objectives should be as general as the client and you are comfortable allowing. The more specific they are, the more that external variables, over which you (and some-

Action Items

times even the client) have no control can influence the outcome. For example, "increasing sales over the current year's total" is a very general objective, and "increasing sales by 11% over this year's total" is a very specific one. An objective in between the two might be "increase sales over last year's total by a minimum of 4% and with a goal of 11%."

I don't like any of those objectives as stated. I'd prefer "maximize sales percentage increase over prior year." Even if you aim for 11% and are successful, how do you know (and how does the client know) it shouldn't have been 26%? I once worked with a firm whose "mantra" for the year was "5% sales increase in the Northeast." At the end of the year, how did they do? They got their 5% increase, and everyone was paid accordingly. Unfortunately, in that economy, with their product, and with the still-struggling competition, they could have increased Northeast sales by at least 40%. Their own objective limited their success.

> Objectives are the key element in the proposal: They establish boundaries, generate the direction of the effort, and set the stage for establishing value (and, therefore, fees).

Specific objectives can also be undermined by truly unforeseen and/or uncontrollable circumstances:

- Key performers leave due to illness, job offers, or career shifts. (In brokerage, real estate, consulting, advertising, and other industries, it's not uncommon for a key executive to leave and take a dozen or more key subordinates along.)

- Major customers go out of business or cut back. (Tough economies force antiquated plants to shut down. All of the businesses trying to keep that plant functional, from water treatment to pollution control, simply lose a customer, usually in an industry where market share is all-important.)

- Competitors introduce new and unanticipated technologies. (No one in the vacuum tube business successfully entered the transistor business which was to make them obsolete.)

- Key information was incorrect. (Apple couldn't meet its sales goals because of inventory deficiencies caused by sales people deliberately underestimating future sales in

order to maximize their commissions for exceeding quotas.)

- Your client is acquired, merges, or undergoes a change in senior management which drastically alters strategies and market tactics. (Many of Chrysler's internal initiatives were curtailed or halted as soon as the Daimler-Benz merger was initiated.)[3]

> Objectives are, ideally, a limited number of business outcomes that are of critical importance to the buyer and under your joint control to achieve. If you can assist in achieving them, you should be seen as a hero (or at least as a competent consultant).

So, objectives should be business outcomes, avoid overly specific minimum standards, and be fairly limited in number. Why limited? Because any project with 23 objectives will not be successful. When everything is a priority, then nothing is a priority. I've seen—and been a part of—major projects with only three or four objectives. After all, "improve our market share to the maximum extent possible" is a pretty hefty piece of work. You don't need a lot more to be said. As a guideline, you're getting overly ambitious once you exceed about six for any particular project.

Finally, I favor bullet points to list the objectives. That's because they are much easier to focus on (and subject to far less misinterpretation) than a narrative, and enable the consultant and the client to have a short list that can be readily communicated to others.

Here are some objectives for our Hewlett-Packard example. Place a check mark next to those which you think best serve the client and the project.

___ Evaluate current duplication of recruiting efforts.

___ Increase long-term retention of all new hires.

___ Reduce costs through elimination of unnecessary vacated positions.

___ Assess cost of each new hire by origin of candidacy.

___ Improve the return on our hiring investment using objective measurement.

---

[3] This point is the key reason to always try to be paid in advance, which we'll discuss below. Proposals should be structured to protect the consultant as much as possible from such variables.

Action Items

__ Reduce costs of recruiting by a minimum of 7% over this year's budget.

__ Reduce recruiting costs company-wide.

__ Analyze job requirements before filling vacant positions.

__ Establish a collaboration in recruiting.

__ Improve productivity by aligning candidate skills with actual job demands.

__ Provide an ongoing measure of recruiting success.

My candidates:

__ Evaluate current duplication of recruiting efforts. (This assumes a cause and assumes that the cause is bad.)

✓ Increase long-term retention of all new hires.

✓ Reduce costs through elimination of unnecessary vacated positions.

__ Assess cost of each new hire by origin of candidacy. (Fails the "So what?" test. This is also an input. It's purely administrative.)

✓ Improve the return on our hiring investment using objective measurement.

__ Reduce costs of recruiting by a minimum of 7% over this year's budget. (Overly specific on the amount. What would happen if a new market campaign demanded that the company increase its employment by 30%? The budget *should* increase in that case.)

✓ Reduce recruiting costs company-wide.

__ Analyze job requirements before filling vacant positions. (Another input with no immediate business outcome as expressed.)

__ Establish a collaboration in recruiting. (So what?)

✓ Improve productivity by aligning candidate skills with actual job demands.

__ Provide an ongoing measure of recruiting success. (This is a metric that will have to be provided, but measuring your success is not in and of itself an objective. It's a natural part of the project that will be described in the next part of the proposal.)

3. Measures of success

Once you've established the business outcomes, you can now ask, "How will we know our progress, and how will we know when we achieved the objectives?" These are important questions, because the answers will indicate that the project is completed.

I've provided questions to ask in the prior chapter. Once again, using a bullet point format, we can list measures of success for our project:

- No new hires depart within the first 90 days stating that "the job isn't what was explained to me." (Currently this occurs 3–4 times a quarter in exit interviews.)

- Recruiting and hiring costs decline in the following measured areas: new hire turnover within the first year; remedial training requests for new hires who should have come on board fully qualified; and work absences of all kinds for new hires during their first year.

- Reduction in number of titled positions over the next year due to attrition and analysis that justifies eliminating the job.

- Focus group and survey results of employees after one year and two years of employment indicate happiness with the position and validate that recruitment, hiring, and orientation were consistent and supportive of their needs.

Note that these measures can be significantly different, depending on what's important to the buyer, what metrics may already exist, and any new metrics that the two of you decide are appropriate. For example, you may have decided to institute a new budget category for all departments to separate out the costs of recruiting and hiring which had previously been lumped under one item in the human resource budget.

All organizations have standard measures in place to evaluate their daily efficiency: sales, profit, response time, inventory, lost job time, equipment down time, market share, etc. There are also the not so easily quantifiable measures that every buyer can cite. For example, I'll know my teamwork is better if I'm spending less time acting as referee for my subordinates. I'll know that morale has improved when I get volunteers for overtime instead of having to order people to stay. And I'll know the environment is improved when I see employees picking up litter they find in the hall and improving their individual work spaces.

> Measuring doesn't have to be done with rocket science precision. It simply has to be done sufficiently to inform the buyer and consultant that progress is being made.

Action Items

As long as you know *who* is doing the measuring and you agree that it's a valid measure, you have your metric.

Thus far we've briefly described the project scenario, listed the results-based objectives, and delineated the way we'll measure progress. Now it's time to reaffirm the value.

4. Expression of value

At this point, I recommend that you reaffirm the value *to the client organization* that was established during the conceptual agreement phase. Remember that both clearly quantifiable criteria *and* subjective, qualitative criteria are acceptable, as long as you agree on who will be the determinant. Here are some examples:

Quantifiable:

- A sales increase of at least 5% within current cost parameters would provide a pre-tax, net profit of about $750,000.

- Reducing the time you spend playing "referee" because your subordinates are not acting as a team would represent a savings of about 20% of your time to spend on strategic issues, which you estimate at about $200,000.

Subjective:

- An improvement in our desk clerks' courtesy and handling of common complaints would generate far better word-of-mouth and consequent repeat business than we have ever enjoyed before.

- Reducing the stress level on the senior management team by implementing a planning process that doesn't immediately put us "in the hole" on January 1 would be simply invaluable.

Here are some specific examples for the Hewlett-Packard proposal we've been working on:

- An improvement of the organization's image in the marketplace would tremendously improve our ability to attract, hire, and retain top-flight talent.

- Reducing turnover of professional hires below current levels during the first year of employment would cut training, hiring, absence, litigation, severance, and related costs by $43,000 per hire. (You estimate that this figure could be reduced conservatively by a total of 200 hires company-wide, representing $8,600,000 in potential savings on this aspect alone.)

- Achieving a coordinated approach to the post-acquisition marketplace and avoiding our current duplication of effort would save us approximately $250,000 a year at current rates.

- Focusing management time and effort on business objectives and strategic goals, avoiding the "failure work" now demanded by replacing people too frequently or performing the work required of unfilled positions.

- Elimination of jobs before they are "mindlessly" filled as soon as they are vacated, through an analysis of job need. You foresee the elimination of about 5% of vacated jobs over the next two years if this were done systematically, representing a savings through this attrition of approximately $1,700,000, comprising salaries, fringes, and recruiting costs saved.

Summary to this point in the process

Let's take a moment to summarize where we are in our acquisition process by using the graphic in Figure 3-1:

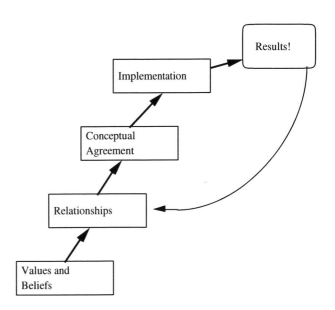

Fig. 3–1: Core consulting process

In our prior discussions with the economic buyer, we've established a common ground of values and beliefs about our approach to the work and the workplace. We then developed a relationship with the buyer based on trust and "free" value delivered early in the discussions. That enabled us to achieve conceptual agreement about the objectives (business outcomes), metrics (measurement of progress toward the outcomes), and value (both in terms

Action Items

of project contribution and our own contribution). *The written proposal we are submitting is a summation of that conceptual agreement provided for the purposes of a formal acknowledgment of what has previously been agreed upon, as well as an expression of other, related details, such as logistics and payment terms.*

Nowhere in Figure 3-1 does the formal step of "proposal acceptance" or, heaven forfend, "fees" appear. These are simply assumptive steps following the key points of objectives, measures, and value.

Now let's return to our proposal creation.

5. Methodologies and options

This is the place where we provide the buyer with the "choice of yeses." We explain the various methodologies employed, and the range of value options available to the buyer.

> The psychological difference between "should I do business with Alan" and "how should I do business with Alan" is enormous. We can significantly influence that dynamic in the proposal with value options.

Methodologies are the techniques employed to gain progress toward the objectives. They may be highly informal and generic, such as interviews, focus groups, observations of company operations, and so forth. Or, they may be formal, specific, and proprietary, including such devices as a particular strategic model, an off-site team building program, a psychometric test, etc. Many methodologies—such as 360° feedback programs—can be proprietary, in that a licensed approach and computer model are used, or generic, in that the consultant may simply interview the appropriate people constituting the feedback group and report the results.

Note: Provide overviews of methodology, but not precise "amounts." In other words, you may specify that focus groups will be used, but you needn't specify there will 14 or 24. Those details can change, and you don't want to create expectations by amount of days or labor. Also, don't worry about "giving away the store." There really is noting new under the sun, and you have a trusting relationship your buyer isn't going to steal your approaches.

This is the advantage of dealing with economic buyers and not feasibility buyers, by the way.

Options are different routes available to the client to meet the same objectives. If your objective is to travel from New York to Philadelphia, the options include a short plane ride, a longer train trip, or a two-hour drive. The plane is the most expensive investment, but it has the distinct value of being faster. The train requires more time, but it has the value of departing and arriving from the center of each city. The car is the most uncomfortable, especially in rush hour, but it has the value of flexibility and a guaranteed departure time.

Note that options are not phases. They are not sequential. Each stands alone. Any option, minimally, can meet the client's objectives (arriving in Philadelphia). The critical difference among options is that the buyer can determine how much benefit he or she chooses to seek in return for various investments. The buyer is making an ROI decision in the midst of the proposal.

Since we want the options to be assessed on value first, they are presented without attendant investment in this section. Psychologically, when presented with three or more options, buyers seldom choose the least valuable (and, consequently, the least expensive) even though it would minimally meet the objectives. This is because:

- No one is comfortable choosing the least value among options.

- Value, if presented well, will overcome cost objections.

- Ego is involved. Buyers believe they get what they pay for. (Don't you?)

Here are some examples of options for our Hewlett-Packard proposal.

Option One:

We will review and analyze the recruiting process now in place, retain the key effective commonalities, and introduce techniques that include behavioral interviewing, computer-assisted candidate elicitation, outsourced reference checks, and a "pre-employment offer orientation" to ensure high quality, well-informed candidates. We will recommend the job positions which should require interviewers, and educate those people in the system and techniques being implemented. We will work with human resources to centralize the quantitative aspects (i.e., reference checks, medical histories), while ensuring the qualitative aspects (i.e., skill fit, behavioral compatibility with the culture) remain in the local hiring unit. Finally, we will implement a system that enables every department

Action Items

manager who has a vacancy to analyze the existing job requirements, the future job requirements, and to assess whether that job should be filled as it exists, merged with other jobs, or eliminated.

Option Two:

In addition to option one interventions, we will educate the human resource department and/or internal consulting teams in the skills necessary to support internal clients in the process of job analysis, candidate attraction and interviewing, and new-hire assimilation. These internal resources may be utilized on an "as needed" basis (reactively) or as an ongoing initiative (proactively) to continually improve the system. This will aid in the goal of making this overall improvement an ongoing process rather than a one time event. In this way, you may choose to conduct job analyses of existing positions even though they are not vacant, and determine how to reassign personnel from those positions deemed no longer necessary in their current form. This would result in additional savings in terms of both eliminated, obsolete jobs and the ability to reassign existing talent to new positions rather than hire new people.

Option Three:

In addition to either option one or two, we will conduct a semiannual audit for two years. On those four occasions we will examine, longitudinally, the effectiveness of job elimination, new hire retention, and new hire effectiveness. We will also recommend ways to continue to improve your internal job analyses from our ongoing client experiences. Our report to you will include measures that you should consider to more accurately gauge your own success in key areas.

6. Timing

Timing simply indicates when you expect to start and when you expect to be finished. Always use calendar dates, so that there is no ambiguity.[4]

The statement may look like this:

Barring unforeseen scheduling problems, we are prepared to begin this project on March 3. We anticipate

---

[4] For example, when you say that a report will be provided 30 days after interviews are completed, the client and you may disagree on when the interviews were completed. The client might use the formal ending date for interviews, while you might be using the date that the final stragglers were finally corralled.

that it will be completed no later than November 1 and, depending on our ability to rapidly schedule key meetings and activities, as early as October 1. In the event either of us encounters unanticipated problems, we will work together to resolve them as expeditiously as possible, and we commit to inform you of any such problems as soon as they occur.

In this manner, you are providing the client with reasonable information to manage the project (and the business) during its life. You've provided a range, because none of us is a perfect forecaster, and you've indicated how you'll handle potential delays.

7. Joint Accountabilities

This section spells out the nature of the partnership. It's important not only to specify "who does what to whom," but also to convey that both consultant and client are accountable for the steps leading to success.

Typically included for the consultant:

- Hold details in confidence, sign nondisclosure agreement
- Agree not to work for direct competition without permission
- Specify which associates will conduct work
- Meet project deadlines
- Inform client immediately of unanticipated problems/ resistance
- Keep client apprised of status
- Submit reports as agreed
- Carry appropriate insurance coverage

Typically included for the client:

- Meet payment terms as specified
- Provide access to people and information as agreed or requested
- Provide logistical support, meeting rooms, facilities, administration, etc.
- Agree to extend schedules if client cannot meet time frames
- Reimburse expenses as agreed
- Apprise consultant of internal changes affecting project
- Respond to inquiries, calls promptly
- Provide clear sponsorship and support where required

Action Items

For our project above, this segment might look like this:

We agree to provide Alan Weiss to conduct all interviews, observations, and other duties, and he will constitute the sole "filter" and single professional contact for your people. If classroom education is desired among the options, we will provide the instructors and materials, subject to your prior review. We will keep you apprised of ongoing progress on a weekly basis, and of crises or unexpected events on an immediate basis. We will maintain full errors and omissions (malpractice) coverage, and will sign nondisclosure agreements as you may require. We will agree not to work with direct competitors for one year without your prior approval.

You agree to provide access to all key personnel and information required to conduct and complete this project. You will return our calls, inquiries, and requests for approvals within 24 hours. You will provide all on-site and off-site logistical support, including classrooms if needed, meeting rooms, scheduling resources, and related help. You agree to pay the fees stipulated within the time frames described, and to reimburse expenses upon their submission. You will inform us immediately of any internal changes which may affect the successful completion of this project.

You may wish to include literal "join accountabilities" for the both of you, e.g., "We will both meet all deadlines as specified or inform the other well in advance if this cannot be accomplished."

8. Terms and conditions

This segment details the fees and how they are paid. This is probably the first time the client has seen the actual fees relevant to each option. It's important that they appear here *after* the original conceptual agreement has been reiterated through the earlier parts of the proposal, and after the options have been explained and reviewed for their relative merits.

Terms and conditions usually include:

- Fees for each option
- Payment terms and timing
- Expenses included and excluded and how they are reimbursed
- Any guarantees you wish to make
- Any demands you wish to make (e.g., noncancellation)
- Any discount options

For this project:

Option 1:	$72,000
Option 2:	$91,000
Option 3, added to either 1 or 2:	$36,000

We require a 50% deposit on signing, with the balance due in 60 days. Alternatively, you may avail yourself of a 10% professional discount if you elect to pay the entire fee at the time of signing.

Expenses will be billed monthly as actually accrued, and reimbursement is due upon presentation of our invoice. Reasonable travel expenses will include hotel, coach class air fare, rental car, taxis, tips, and meals. All other expenses, such as fax, courier, phone, duplication, administrative work, etc., are included in our fees.

Our work is guaranteed. If we do not meet the mutually agreed upon objectives within the time frames specified, we will continue to work on the project at no additional fee until they are met. If we are unable to meet them within a reasonable time after that determination, we will refund your full fee. In return, this project is non-cancellable for any reason. Payments are due as specified. However, you may delay and reschedule this project at any time without penalty, subject to mutually agreeable future dates.[5]

(Note: You don't have to include all of these provisions, discounts, etc. However, what you see above is a classic *quid pro quo*: A guarantee of work to be performed in return for a non-cancellation clause. Many consultants prefer a cancellation policy with penalties.)

> Terms and conditions should be straightforward and free of "boilerplate." If the proposal goes to the legal department, it means two things: You don't have a strong relationship with the buyer, and the proposal will not return looking like it did when you sent it.

---

[5] Note that I don't advocate a "good until" date, because proposals based on conceptual agreement with a true buyer don't sit around for a year, and I don't want to imply that I'm willing to wait that long anyway. See Chapter Five for a discussion of how to effectively follow up.

Action Items

9. Acceptance

It's good to get a signature while you can, so include that provision at the end of your proposal document. Here's a simple format:

Acceptance

This proposal is accepted and forms an agreement between Hewlett-Packard, Inc. (you) and Summit Consulting Group, Inc. (we/us/I) as represented by Alan Weiss. Alternatively, your deposit will represent your agreement to all terms specified.

For Summit Consulting   For Hewlett-Packard, Inc.:
Group, Inc.:

Alan Weiss   _____
President

                                 _____

Date: August 16, 1999   Date:_____

(I find that many buyers can authorize a check but can't sign a contract without the legal department's approval, and they detest that involvement as much as I do. Hence, the alternative of acceptance with a payment, which several of my clients have readily embraced.)

Quick Start: Use the proposal above, or in the appendix, or on the CD to create your own template on your computer, and simply fill in the content. This will save considerable time and effort. And make sure you also maintain it on your lap top, so that you can readily produce proposals while traveling, while the issues are timely and urgent.

Summary of Chapter 3:

- There are nine components to a successful proposal.

- Situation appraisals are meant to briefly reestablish conceptual agreement.

- Objectives are the most critical element, and must be outcome-based.

- Measures of success can be objective or subjective, as long as you agree on the measurement device.

- A choice of options—of "yeses"—will significantly improve the probability of acceptance of any proposal.

- Acceptance should be immediately available to the buyer at the conclusion of the proposal.

Action Items

Interlude: Finding the Hidden Personal Objectives

Logic makes people think, but emotions make them act. Hence, tightly conceived intellectual arguments will seldom result in high quality conceptual agreement. With rare exception (lawyers and engineers, perhaps), buyers are most amenable to new approaches and most malleable when viscerally involved.

The secret which few people understand is that the emotional connection is only superficially about business and organizational objectives. Behind virtually every such objective is a *personal objective* which really constitutes the buyer's nerve ending and most visceral contact.

If you don't believe that, think about this: In the most aggressive business campaigns and initiatives, employees will resist the prescribed path if they perceive pain or discomfort, or even ennui. Sales people have notoriously resisted new approaches if they feel there is more work, increased risk, or decreased status.

So, no matter how gung-ho the buyer may feel about corporate goals, the most efficacious propulsion will be a simultaneous appeal to individual betterment.

Here are some examples of corporate business objectives and representative personal objectives which can lurk just underneath them:

Corporate:	Personal:
• Improve teamwork	• End my role as unpopular arbiter
• Increase retention	• Free up my time from recruiting demands
• Increase sales	• Maximize my incentive compensation
• Decrease attrition	• End the pressure of constantly seeking business
• Conflict resolution	• Alleviate my stress levels
• Strategic planning	• End my uncertainty and ambiguity
• Coaching/development	• Improve my repute and regard by others
- Improve communications	- Help me influence others faster
- Enhance quality control	- Get the plant manager off my back

When you're pursuing conceptual agreement, your relationship-building, after all, is with the buyer, not the corporate entity. The resultant trust is with the buyer, not the bricks and mortar. Ideally, then, the objectives become an amalgam of the legitimate needs of the organization and the equally valid needs of the individual. I am going to support a corporate initiative that clearly and directly enhances my well being much more assiduously than one which is remote or unrelated to my well being. This isn't selfish, it's merely human nature.

How do you unearth these personal objectives without seeming to make a mercenary appeal to bald self-interest (and, probably, alienate the buyer)? As with most aspects of proposal-building, you do it with questions.

First, here are some typical questions you ask the buyer to elicit organizational objectives:

• What would you like to accomplish?

• What would the ideal results be?

• How will behavior be changed?

• How will customers be impacted?

• How will conditions be improved?

• What standards will be raised?

• What new results will accrue?

• What ROI (ROE/ROA/ROS, etc.) is desired?

• What new efficiencies will prevail?

• How will the product, service, and/or relationship be enhanced?

Now, here are some parallel questions which you can weave in to determine the buyer's stake and desired personal improvement:

Action Items

- How will this impact you, personally?

- How does this impact your own performance?

- What opportunity does this afford you?

- How will your life be different as a result?

- To what degree will this reflect directly on you?

- How will the result affect your stress level?

- What impact will this success have on your time?

- To what extent will this provide you with more latitude/flexibility?

- Why are you willing to champion, support, and fund this?

- What are the risks and rewards awaiting you in this area?

You don't have to ask all the questions, of course, but a representative sample will lead you to the key emotional triggers for that buyer, personally.

Action Items

Chapter Four

Eleven Golden Rules for Presenting a Proposal

Eleven Golden Rules for Presenting a Proposal

1. Get it there fast.

2. Make sure it is error-free.

3. Ensure a faithful rendition of the conceptual agreement.

4. Keep it relatively brief.

5. Provide multiple copies.

6. Sign it in the acceptance segment.

7. Place it in a presentation folder or other appropriate package.

8. Enclose something of value (no, not a bribe).

9. Use hard copy, not e-mail or fax.

10. Provide a brief cover letter.

11. Specify the next step very clearly.

1. Get it there fast

Let's not beat around the bush. Since a proposal, ideally, is a *summation of conceptual agreement*, the best way to present it is as quickly as possible. That means a FedEx[1] package preferably the next day but certainly within 48 hours. The longer you wait, the more things can go wrong. Strike while conceptual agreement is hot and momentum is in your favor.

The longer you wait, the more you risk:

• Unexpected event (buyer's child breaks a leg).

• Subordinate raises an objection.

• Another alternative (someone's cousin) is introduced.

• Someone reads something that clouds the issue.

• The buyer's boss enters the picture.

• The company circumstances change (merger, poor sales, volcano).

• The problem is suddenly perceived to be solved.

• A larger problem appears, dwarfing the one you were addressing.

• The prospect's competition drops a bombshell.

• The strong relationship with the buyer waning.

You get the idea. Always try to have office time (even on the road) immediately after a call that you even guess will result in a request for a proposal. (You can usually tell if you've been meeting with the economic buyer, conceptual agreement is gaining momentum, a sense of urgency is being conveyed, etc.). It's very powerful to be able to say, "I'll have the proposal on your desk tomorrow morning" (or, in worst case, the day after tomorrow). If you can't arrange such office time, or the prospect surprises you with quick conceptual agreement, use modern technology to create the proposal. In other words, have your lap top with you, use e-mail to have someone in your office create it for you, dictate it by phone if you have to. This is simply a factual observation and not a value judgment: Speed often determines acceptance, just as rain often postpones a ball game. You might not like that fact, but there it is. And, in this electronic age, there really is no reason to be dilatory.

If you follow the methodical, brief approach we've described earlier in this book, it's relatively simple to produce an excellent proposal quickly and flawlessly.

Don't forget, despite the conceptual agreement, the prospect is seeing two things for the first time in your written proposal: 1) the options you are suggesting, and 2) the actual fees. That's why it's so important to put this document in front of the buyer while conceptual agreement is still hot and prior to other factors intervening.

---

[1] Folks, there simply isn't anyone as good as FedEx, and saving money on sending a proposal is like looking for the best deal in brain surgeons. You simply want the one who does it best.

Action Items

> There is some doubt that Confederate
> General Nathan Bedford Forrest
> actually explained his success by saying,
> "I get there firstest with the mostest,"
> but the point needed to be made.

2. Make sure it is error-free

This might seem like a no-brainer, but it's not.[2] The best way to ensure an error-free proposal is to have at least two other people read it. If you're a solo practitioner, that means using family and friends, as necessary.

Here are the "usual suspects" which undermine your proposal:

- Spelling errors. Don't be lulled by spell-checkers on your computer. They don't normally discriminate, for example, between "there," "they're," and "their."[3] If you must check the spelling by yourself, read the document backwards, which forces you *not* to assume the meaning and rush onward, even though you wrote the words.

- Grammar and punctuation errors. I have heard buyers explain that they rejected a proposal because English wasn't used properly. There is a difference between "imply" and "infer," for example, and if you're not sure what it is, either look it up or don't use that construction. Tenses are commonly used incorrectly (e.g., "none is" is correct, while "none are" is not). A comma and period always go inside a quote ("." or ",") no matter what the logic of the sentence, while a colon and semi-colon always go outside a quote. There are no exceptions. Might a prospect be this fussy? Do you want to take the chance with something that can be so readily avoided?

- Buyer's name, rank, and serial number. *Always* get the buyer's business card sometime during your meetings. If you can't get that right, can the buyer expect you to get the project right?

- Technical jargon. Every company has technical abbreviations, in-house jargon, and acronyms in its daily vernacular. Just because you've heard them doesn't ensure that you either understand them or can spell them. If you're not sure, ask. If you're still not sure, avoid them. Merck talks about "Docs," meaning physicians, although one of my colleagues thought it meant "documents." Is someone referring to trouble with their "e-mail" or "v-mail" systems? State Street executives kept mentioning "SSGA" and "custody" and other parochial terms. I didn't want to bring the conversation to a halt by constantly demanding simultaneous translation, so I made a note of *anything* I wasn't sure about and asked one of the secretaries later on. They're happy to be of help, and they know *everything* because they usually have to type it.[4]

- Sloppy formatting. If you're using sub-heads (which you would be if you followed my examples) in the proposal, make sure they don't begin at the bottom of a page. Use a page-break. Ensure that you're consistent: What's bold in one spot should be bold in another, and a category calling for italics should consistently be in italics. Place page numbers in the footer. Use fonts and type sizes that are easy to read and logical. For example, sans serif fonts are good for large headlines, but not copy, which is better read with serif fonts. Here's an example:

Objectives:

1. Improve image in the marketplace through mass media.

"Objectives" is in a 14 point Helvetica bold type, while the line under it is in 12 point Bookman.

> You never know what turns off a buyer.
> You do know that errors and sloppiness
> are likely suspects, so why run
> the risk? After months of building
> a relationship, do you want to
> ruin it in one day?

3. Ensure a faithful rendition of the conceptual agreement

Interweave your situation appraisal, objectives, measures for success, and value statements with expressions such as:

---

[2] I know a consultant who spelled the name "USAir" incorrectly (before it became US Airways) and was miffed that this prospect was upset and rejected the proposal out of hand!

[3] Yes, I know there are grammar checkers, but they are so flawed that they usually require far more time than they're worth.

[4] Similarly, if you're ever uncertain while off-site, call the switchboard. Receptionists are also omniscient.

Action Items

- As we discussed . . .
- Per your suggestion . . .
- In our meeting of the 14th . . .
- Your point about . . .
- Our prior agreement was that . . .
- We had stipulated that . . .
- We had agreed in prior correspondence that . . .
- As you recall . . .
- My understanding of our agreement is . . .
- You had specifically mentioned that . . .
- You specified that . . .
- My earlier summary, with which you agreed, said . . .
- Consistent with the reports that we reviewed . . .

You get the idea. You want to constantly remind the buyer that all of this has been agreed upon (which is why I advocate beginning the entire proposal with a situation appraisal). The method behind this madness is that the prospect should be in a fine frame of agreement by the time he or she gets to the key juncture: the options and fees you are presenting *in light of that prior agreement.*

It's important that you both make and review the notes of your prior meetings carefully. Often, notes taken in haste during meetings are unrecognizable a few days later. Review your notes right after a meeting and annotate those parts that are hard to read. In preparing your proposal, religiously consult:

- Notes taken during meetings.
- Notes made during telephone calls.
- All prospect correspondence, in either direction.
- All background materials provided by the prospect.
- Your memory of any and all related matters.
- Material you've gathered from other sources.[5]
- Your phone book—don't be hesitant to make a call to clarify any vague points or indecipherable notes.

Remind the prospect as often as tactfully possible that most of this is simply a reiteration of what both of you believe must be done.

[5] You should be gathering *Wall Street Journal* articles, magazine pieces, public reports, etc.

> Although you hate to believe it, the buyer is dealing with a lot more pressing issues than merely your proposed project. Reminding the buyer of your "history" isn't hounding, but simply good reporting.

4. Keep it relatively brief

We stated earlier that a fine proposal seldom needs to be longer than two or three pages. The buyer doesn't have all that much time, and it's much simpler to approve something that can be digested in a few minutes than something that takes all day, three other people, and a legal opinion to comprehend.

Enough said?

5. Provide multiple copies

The buyer needs a minimum of two copies: one for the company, and one to return (presumably signed) to you. However, there might be ample reason for even more copies:

- The buyer's boss
- Interested (and important) subordinates
- Concerned colleagues
- Working copies to hand out as needed
- Copies required for legal, accounting, purchasing, etc.

My habit is to indicate that two copies will be provided, but that I can send as many as required. In an age of photocopiers that may seem unnecessary, but think of it this way: It may be political to have "original" copies with your signature on them to distribute, rather than documents from the photocopier. Consequently, your copies should be "originals" off your computer and not off your copy machine.

You may "dress this up" a bit, by indicating with a Post-it note "top copy for Ms. Jones" or "first document for Mr. Smith." My habit is *not* to send the proposal to anyone other than the buyer, personally. It's the buyer's choice to whom to send copies, not mine. But I want to provide them in case they're needed, and I want to head off the mi-

Action Items

nor delay that occurs when you hear, "Sorry, but could you provide three more originals so that we can get this processed correctly?" Remember what we said in rule #1, any delay is a potentially fatal delay.

6. Sign it in the acceptance segment

It makes no sense to have a proposal that must be followed by a contract. That particular two-step dance only creates more delay, and leaves you vulnerable to the issues in rule #1. Use your proposal *as a contract.*

Some consultants submit an unsigned proposal. They want the prospect to sign and return it, at which point they will execute it and provide the completed copy to the client. The rationale for this is that you don't want to sign a form that may be changed by the other party before he or she signs. (We all receive contracts like this from publishers, agents, etc.).

The problem with this philosophy is twofold: First, it implies that you don't trust the buyer, especially after building the relationship and, ostensibly, having secured conceptual agreement. Second, it delays the consummation of the agreement still further while the proposal is returned to you and then sent—once again—to the client.

Sign the proposal (on every copy) prior to sending it via FedEx. If the client wants to make some small corrections, allow for them through the initialing of the changes in the margins, once agreed on by phone. (You can mention this in the cover letter. See rule #10.) *If you've provided options as I've advocated in Chapter 3, provide a clear place to select the option of choice.*

Finally, be willing to start work immediately, *prior to the signing of the proposal.* Many clients will say that their internal bureaucracy or chain of command will require a week to process the proposal, but there's an opportunity to begin the project immediately while certain people are in town, a particular event is taking place, or a crisis needs resolution. Accept, eagerly. The luxury of dealing with an economic buyer, with whom you have reached conceptual agreement, is that you can trust each other implicitly.

I always tell clients I'm willing to begin work on a "verbal handshake," and I mean it. Sometimes I'll say, "If the proposal is acceptable and we have a deal, I'm happy to begin immediately. You can return the signed document at your convenience." By acknowledging that statement, the buyer has given you permission to begin the project—not just a part of it—and to commence the billing process immediately. I call this immediate commencement of work "pouring cement on the agreement." *I have often been paid prior to receiving the signed proposal back and, on occasion, it's never been formally signed.*

> Proposals—and their acceptance—are based on trust, not legalities. Sign your copy and agree to proceed on even a telephone approval. The lawyers will tell you this is not prudent, but they're the ones who are still charging by the hour rather than for their value . . .

I don't care. An oral agreement is fine with me, and a check from the client usually signifies that they're highly committed!

7. Place it in a presentation folder or other appropriate package

Don't send the proposal (and attendant copies) by themselves in the courier packaging. They should always be sealed in an envelope, addressed to your buyer, with "confidential" prominently displayed. It's up to the buyer whether a secretary or assistant can open a confidential envelope, but it's incumbent upon you to ensure that the warning is in place. After all, the proposal involves the investment of funds in a project that might be threatening to some people. Marking the inside envelope "personal and confidential" is not overdoing it.

I prefer a presentation folder of some kind, with your cover letter on one side and the proposal copies on the other. You may already be using presentation folders for your media kit, inquiry responses, and/or publicity needs. If you don't, or use a very generic one, it's a good investment to have some printed on good stock with large inside pockets to hold thick documents. You can have these embossed with your company logo at minimum cost, yet they convey a highly professional image and tell the prospect that it's not an "off the shelf" item. Make no mistake: Every piece of your literature and packaging that is seen by the client will convey an image of professionalism (or lack thereof) no matter how insignificant it may seem.[6]

---

[6] This is why my recommendation to new consultants with limited budgets is always to invest in stationery and company literature of very high quality. Never skimp on any material that meets the public. You're much better off with no brochure at all than with an obviously inexpensive one (such as the triple-fold types that fit in #10 envelopes).

Action Items

Now for the minutiae. Make sure the proposal pages are numbered, even if there are only two or three of them. Staple each set. Sometimes folders are dropped or loose sheets migrate across an executive's desk. You don't want someone reading a proposal with a page missing or a duplicate of the same page. It seems like a minor matter, but why risk it if the stapler can take care of it in less than a second?

So: Multiple sets of the proposal on one side of a presentation folder with a cover letter on the other side; the folder ensconced in an envelope marked "confidential"; the envelope inside a FedEx courier envelope with the buyer's personal address, mail stop, and phone number on the air bill. Keep your copy of the air bill and call two days later to ensure that it was received. That's a good technique for a nonassertive follow up (but see Rule #11).

> Everything you send to a prospect reflects on your image and professionalism. People do judge books—and proposals— by their covers.

8. Enclose something of value (no, not a bribe)

I've found it to be highly effective to enclose something with the proposal. I usually use some idea or request I've picked up from the buyer during my conversations, and have made a note that it would be an appropriate enclosure when it's time to submit the proposal.

The philosophy is simple. You want to continue the sequence of trust, sharing, and value generation that has been established during prior conversations and interactions. In other words, the proposal that's enclosed is simply a confirmation of what's previously been discussed and decided, and there are some other things of interest here, as well.

Appropriate enclosures might include:

• A book or article you've written that has been cited earlier.

• A book or article by someone else that is relevant to the project.

• An example of findings or surveys from other firms.[7]

• A seminar or convention announcement of interest.

• An industry report.

• A software review or recommendation (but not the software itself).

• A personal or lifestyle idea (e.g., a vacation spot you've discussed).[8]

• Additional ideas for the project the client can implement alone.

• Information about a client goal (e.g., expansion in Europe).

• Web sites that have helpful content.

Your cover letter can refer to the fact that you've also enclosed an item which you thought would be of interest, which you had promised earlier, which you've finally received after a delay, or which just came to your attention. This is an example of continuing to provide value. The subliminal effect can be powerful.

After all, this is not just about a proposal. It's about a *relationship*.

9. Use hard copy, not e-mail or fax

In some instances, a prospect will indicate that there's an urgency to get a proposal in front of someone rapidly, or that the buyer is about to leave on a trip and would like to take your proposal along to review. Often, a prospect will simply say "fax me your proposal" or will send an e-mail with an invitation to reply via the same medium.

There is seldom the situation where an overnight delivery doesn't serve the purposes of urgency. However, the means above are not mutually-exclusive. If you absolutely have to send a fax or e-mail, follow it up with hard copy shipped via courier (do not resort to the normal mails simply because you've sent an electronic copy).

Hard copy looks better. It can be more readily handed to others in a professional form. E-mail will often lose formatting, and will always lose the effectiveness of your logo and look. Faxes are often hard to read and sometimes

---

[7] Naturally, these would have to be non-proprietary and non-confidential.

[8] I once provided a chamber of commerce guide to the city where the buyer's daughter had just been accepted to college.

Action Items

lose detail around the edges. And faxes and e-mail are notoriously unsecure.

In 90% of the cases, overnight service will be faster than expected. In the other 10%, if the request is legitimate, back up the fax or e-mail with overnight hard copy. Emphasize in the e-mail or fax that hard copy is arriving the next day. A faxed or e-mailed proposal simply does not look as professional and loses a great deal of its impact. In addition, you can't enclose anything of value in electronic communications or faxes other than suggestions or scanned copies.

10. Provide a brief cover letter

The cover letter should be a single page. It should refer to the proposal, the fact that it's expected, any other enclosures (value) you've provided, and any details that you want to conversationally convey, including any items from the first nine rules (e.g., that the buyer may make minor corrections right on the document).

Here is a sample.

January 1, 2000
Mr. Glenn Davis
Vice President, Operations
Global Worldwide, Inc.
Box 1000
New York, NY 10000

Dear Glenn:

I've enclosed the proposal we've discussed. You'll find that it summarizes the points raised in our meetings of December 2 and 12, particularly the objectives, measures of success, and value of attaining those objectives.

In reviewing our tentative plans, I developed three options which may be of interest. Any of them can meet the objectives, but some provide for additional value, and I wanted you to be able to make as flexible an investment/return decision as possible. I'm prepared to work on whichever option you prefer.

If there are minor alterations required to the proposal, feel free to make them and initial them on the copy you return. Should you have any uncertainties about changes, feel free to give me a call at any time. In fact, I'm prepared to begin the project based on your verbal "handshake" should you want to get started prior to the paperwork being processed. Simply indicate which option you've chosen, and I can be on site to begin the initial planning meeting as early as Monday of next week.

I've also enclosed a survey report from the Global Trade Council on lessons learned from expansion in Asia. I requested this for you some time ago and it's finally arrived. I marked a chart on page six that seems especially pertinent to your strategy regarding Singapore.

Thanks so much for considering me for this project. If I don't hear from you prior, I'll call on Friday at 10 am to ensure that you've received this and to respond to any questions. I'm looking forward to working with you.

Alan Weiss, Ph.D.
President
AW/mg
Enc.

Note the assumptive closing at the end. It never hurts.

One more suggestion: Enclose a self-addressed, paid envelope[9] of appropriate size, or a courier air bill from your account. I often do this with invoices. It can prompt a speedier return, and it always ensures that nothing is lost in the mail.

11. Specify the next step very clearly

Make it clear what the next step is. I've indicated above that I'll call on a specific date at a specific time. It's a good idea to establish such follow up even earlier, before leaving the client. Too many consultants reach the "home stretch" and don't cross the finish line because they assume that the buyer will dutifully contact them. You must create the expectation, obligation, and date for this to occur.

This small step will eliminate a great deal of the chronic complaint, "Why won't they get back to me?!"

Quick Start: Read your proposal **from the buyer's point of view** *before sending it. Make sure that it is clear and not merely a parochial view from your perspective. You might want to have a third party read it if possible.*

Summary of Chapter 4:

- There are eleven "Golden Rules" for presenting a proposal.

- Speed may not be everything, but it counts for a great deal.

---

[9] The most professional way to do this is with a post office account that allows you to print envelopes with your return mail permit right on them.

Action Items

- Submit a signed, completed proposal that can be used immediately to launch the project without further delay.

- Trust is the key to acceptance, not a legal contract covering every possible contingency.

- Content is crucial, but image is also important.

- Provide additional value with the proposal.

- Include a cover letter that confirms a follow-up.

Self-Assessment Questions:

1. How fast do you get the completed proposal to the buyer? Are you able to consistently provide it within 48 hours?

2. Are you proud of the appearance of your proposals in terms of image and professionalism?

3. How many "first hits" do you get, with proposals accepted upon submission without having to make additional changes or revisit the client to review the proposal?

4. Are you sending hard copy proposals, or are you relying on fax and e-mail? (Even if the client requests electronic media, there is no substitute for hard copy.)

5. How often do you send a personalized cover letter that formalizes a follow-up procedure?

Action Items

Chapter Five

How to follow up: What happens after you submit the proposal?

Ah, the agony begins. How long do you wait before demanding to know why the buyer hasn't sent you the first check, yet? Do you confidently call a few days later, or do you wait, aloof and professional, as though all of your other projects were consuming your time?

When to follow up

As cited in the prior chapter, the ideal follow-up is a planned one, which removes all the doubts about timing and also manages the buyer's expectations (as well as creates a small sense of urgency around the decision). There are three ways to accomplish this.

1. In the discussions leading up to the actual creation of the proposal, mention that your habit is to give the buyer a day or two to review the details and options, and then to call at a specific time to respond to any questions and/or to actually begin the project.[1] You merely want to set the stage for your proposal management.

When you are actually ready to prepare the proposal, mention to the buyer the exact time he or she will be receiving it, and check for a good follow-up date. "I'll be sending this via courier so that it arrives on your desk Thursday morning. I'd like to call you between 10 and 12 on Monday to discuss your reaction. Does that fit your schedule?" If the buyer says no, there's a field trip scheduled next week, then ask what a good time would be. Two key criteria:

- You want a phone call (or personal visit), not e-mail or voice mail.

- You want to initiate it (as opposed to the buyer) to ensure positive contact.

If the buyer says, "I'm going on a two-week trip to Europe next week," what's your response?

The response is, "Then why don't I get the proposal to you tomorrow, and call you on Thursday. Would that work better for you?"

With a planned follow-up you've avoided the worry about when to call and you've created a ready-made excuse to cut through any gatekeepers. "This is Dr. Weiss, and Ms. Shane is expecting my call. Yes, I know it's a hectic day, but she and I agreed that this would be our only mutually agreeable time to talk. Could you please let her know I'm on the phone?"

2. Mention your intent in your cover letter.[2] Let the buyer know that you'll be following up at a specified *time and date*. Leave nothing to chance. Invite the buyer to let you know if that arrangement is not agreeable, but stipulate that, unless you hear otherwise, you'll be contacting the buyer at that time.[3] This technique also enables you to say, "I'm calling as agreed." (This phrase will get you past most gatekeepers, and may even convince a secretary to take a moment to track down the buyer, or at least place you on his or her calendar later that day.)

3. Do both 1 and 2. If you constantly reinforce the fact that your normal policy is to submit a proposal rapidly after the conceptual agreement, then follow up promptly for reaction, and then be prepared to launch the actual project quickly, you will create the proper expectations—and, one hopes, behaviors—on the part of the buyer.

> Follow-up should not involve
> another sequence of courtship. It
> should be the arrangements
> for the wedding reception.

---

[1] I'm aware that we haven't covered presenting a proposal in person. That's because it's generally a horrible idea if the buyer hasn't yet seen it and generally wastes a meeting ("Well, thanks for explaining everything, I'll get back to you once I've given it some serious study."). Occasionally, a buyer will request a meeting after the proposal has been received and reviewed, which is a different dynamic.

[2] See Chapter 4 for a sample.

[3] This is as good a place as any to mention that it's always a good idea to get the buyer's private line, private e-mail, and private fax numbers. Early in the relationship, you might provide your home phone number or private line on a card for the buyer, and ask if there is an expeditious way to reach him or her. This usually avoids gatekeepers entirely.

Action Items

What to do when an appearance is required

Sometimes the buyer will say, "We need to discuss this in person, and I'd like to get some other people in on it."

This is good news/bad news. The good news is that the buyer is willing to spend more personal time on the proposal, and wants to give you a chance to close the deal. The bad news is that the proposal itself wasn't sufficient, and that conceptual agreement might not have been as solid as you thought.

Some rules for a personal appearance follow-up:

1. Always accept. Don't try to close on the business by phone.

2. Arrange it as quickly as possible. Remember, the longer the process takes, the more that can go haywire.

3. Ensure that the buyer will be there personally. If he or she will not be, then arrange to see him or her privately before and after the meeting with subordinates.

4. Find out who else, if anyone, will be there. Ask the buyer whether the proposal can be made available to them so that everyone is at the same level of understanding.

5. Ask quite candidly if there are any objections, drawbacks, unexpected developments, or anything else that you should know about and prepare for *in order to make the best use of everyone's time.* Don't wait for an ambush, and then go in unarmed, and then refuse to fight. Determine who will be shooting, from where, and with what, and arm yourself accordingly.

6. Test the status. Ask, "If we can reach agreement at that meeting, are you prepared to proceed?" Try to get the buyer to commit to a proposed course of action, i.e., amend a part of the methodology and we can go on, or shorten the time frame for data gathering and we can probably agree on a start date. *If you're particularly assertive, ask this great question: "What will you and I have to accomplish at that meeting (or you, your colleagues, and I) in order to begin the project?"*

As a rule, the more specific the buyer is in response to point #6, the better your chances. The more vague the buyer sounds, the more trouble awaiting you.

Let's take one item off the table right now: fees. If the buyer says that your fees are too high—for all of your options—*do not offer to lower fees.* That tactic will either lose the business immediately ("Hmmnn, how low can he go?") or will gain you business that you hate ("I'm actually losing money on this deal").[4]

Instead, offer to reduce value. That's right. All buyers want to reduce fees, but they seldom want to reduce value. For example:

"So, you favor option two but don't have the budget for it? Well, we could restrict it to domestic people, and not sample international professionals."

"No, the international people are always complaining that they're left out. We have to include them."

"All right, then why don't we eliminate the post-survey training session for your middle managers?"

"That's no good. If we don't train them to deal with the results of the survey, they'll maintain the behaviors that created the problem to begin with."

"Suppose we don't do the employee feedback meetings?"

"Out of the question. They'll claim we didn't listen, or watered down the actual feedback."

You get the idea. *Keep focusing on buyer results, not on buyer investment.* In many cases, you'll be able to help the buyer to justify "finding" the money needed elsewhere.

> The discussion should never be about fees. It should always be about value. If it's about the former, you've lost control of the situation. This is your fault, not the buyer's.

There are other objections, unrelated to fees, that you might hear, either from the buyer in advance or from the buyer and/or colleagues at the actual meeting. They typically include:[5]

- The timing is too aggressive or too tame.

- Subordinates are threatened by the outside intervention.

- Sensitive political/cultural issues are involved (e.g., compensation).

---

[4] For a detailed study of how to handle fee objections and maximize fee ranges, see my book, *Value-Based Fees,* Jossey-Bass/Pfeiffer, 2002.

[5] Don't forget, all of the forgoing assumes that you've been dealing with the real economic buyer. If subsequent events indicate that the resistance is caused by the fact that your presumed buyer really doesn't have that authority, then you must begin the courtship again by finding out who the real buyer is. You cannot sell anything to gatekeepers or recommenders.

Action Items

- A union is presenting problems.

- Other projects, planned or ongoing, are threatened.

- Something has "come up" unexpectedly.

No matter what the objection, you should use the same tactic: Make the resistance a part of the solution. Don't attempt to smash through it, overcome it heroically, or throw yourself on your sword ("You'll have to trust me on this, I've seen it before, and I'm confident we can overcome it").

Tell the buyer and others that the objection makes sense, and ask what *they would recommend* to overcome it. Tell them that you have some ideas and experience from other clients, but that they know their culture best and you'd be happy to work in their resolutions. At the same time, assure them that there are *always* objections, and that the timing is *never* perfect, and that there will probably be some more stumbling blocks before this is over. Nevertheless, successful projects are launched every day in far worse scenarios than this one and we're all intelligent people here, so let's work out the best resolution we can while we're together.

You want to enlist the ambushers in finding a better trail out of there. Don't shoot back. They're occupying the heights. Ask them to show you the best way up the hill, but be clear that there is always a way up the hill, and your combined vantage points should determine the best path.

I cover this point in depth in several other books, such as *How to Sell New Business and Expand Existing Business*, but let me just mention it here: There is no objection you haven't heard. And the vast majority fall into only four areas: No money, no hurry/urgency, no need, and no trust. Obviously, these should all have been overcome in reaching conceptual agreement. But any objection that does now surface will be in one of those four areas, so prepare yourself accordingly.

To summarize for a "command appearance":

1. Prepare yourself ahead of time with the buyer's input.

2. Take fees off the table and focus on value.

3. Use the resistors to help formulate the solution.

4. Close on the deal.

The final step in follow-up meetings is to summarize the agreements you've collectively reached, and then use this assumptive statement: "Can we work from the current proposal with some modifications initialed by you, or would you prefer an entirely new document? I'm prepared to begin immediately, so what would make the most sense to move us along?"

In the worst case, the buyer will request more time and/or more meetings. In this situation, you've probably lost the deal, though there's still a glimmer. Ask again: "What would we need to do in order to reach final agreement? What haven't we established yet that still requires resolution?" At this stage, that's still time well spent, though decreasingly so. Your buyer might be resisting, despite presumed conceptual agreement, and despite a fine personal meeting, because:

- There are problems which are not being disclosed (e.g., reorganization).

- The buyer intends to tackle your project internally.

- The buyer can't say "no" but doesn't want to say "yes."

- You have misread the situation.

- You don't really have a buyer in front of you, despite your earlier confidence.

A proposal based on sound conceptual agreement probably has an 80% chance of acceptance.[6] That same proposal, when the buyer requests a subsequent meeting with you, is probably at 65%. If nothing is concluded in that meeting, your chances are probably less than 50% for the next two weeks, and virtually nil thereafter.

A personal appearance is still a fine opportunity. But take it very seriously and prepare assiduously: It's probably a "make it or break it" point.

What to do if the buyer is unresponsive

Our worst nightmare in this business is the buyer who mysteriously forgets how to use the phone. I've always preferred a candid, polite "no" to an extended, amateurish dance that results in the same answer. It's one thing to lose a project; it's another to also lose valuable time and resources.

Here's my "escalation sequence" for eliciting a response from a hiding buyer. (Normally, this shouldn't happen if you have a solid relationship and conceptual agreement, and you've specified a certain follow-up date, but it some-

---

[6] Bear in mind that "exploratory" proposals, submitted without conceptual agreement and/or without contact with the real buyer, probably have about a 10% chance of acceptance.

Action Items

times does, nonetheless. Also, these tactics can be used at any point in the sales process, not only post-proposal.) I'm assuming that each step is unsuccessful in eliciting a personal response prior to going to the next one.

1. Make your phone call as planned (agreed upon day).

2. Make a second phone call, with a courteous message (next day).

3. Make a third and final phone call indicating your confusion and indicating that you'll send something in writing (three days later).

4. Simultaneously send an e-mail and letter marked personal and confidential, politely asking for a response so that you can plan your time accordingly and offering to see the buyer personally if desired (one week later).

5. Send a certified letter to the buyer indicating professionally that the proposal terms will be honored only for another 30 days, at which time all terms would have to be reviewed and renegotiated. Indicate that this will be your final letter (two weeks later).

I usually don't go beyond this, because I don't want to throw good money after bad, and I never take it personally. After all, just because your buyer has a personality disorder or is neurotic (one of which is probably the case with these "disappearances") doesn't mean that you're a bad person. Further, psychologically, it's depressing to deal with this passive/aggressive rejection, so it's best to remove ourselves from it, which we're quite capable of doing.

If you want to escalate beyond my steps, however, here is the nuclear arsenal:

6. Ask the secretary if the buyer is sick or anything unexpected has happened, then find out what his or her schedule is. If the buyer is visiting the Philadelphia field office on Friday, for example, you can place a call there and almost assuredly ambush the buyer through a non-suspecting local switchboard operator.

7. Send an invoice to the buyer for your expenses to date (which you should actually absorb as marketing expenses) given the fact that the meetings and interaction were apparently to gain information from you but not to seriously consider a project.

8. Send an invoice for your fee in terms of the value you've provided, per point #7.

9. Send a letter with a copy of the proposal to the buyer's boss. Explain the steps you've taken to try to obtain a response, and that you're worried that your proprietary information, models, material, etc. might be used without

your consent or appropriate payment. Ask if there is some way to resolve the impasse.

10. Send a certified letter to the buyer explaining that the buyer's failure to conform to your agreement for response, and your consequent inability to determine the status of the project (and the material you've provided) means that all agreements are null and void. Therefore, you do not feel constrained to conform to any real or implied nondisclosure about what you've learned, nor will you return any of the proprietary materials the company has provided to you.

I *do not* advocate steps 6 through 10, but you may occasionally be unable to exorcise the demon of the disappearing buyer without resorting to stronger actions. I have met a couple of these people. If you think you're unfortunate for having had to deal with them, think of the great misfortune of their companies, which pay them significant amounts of money in support of unprofessional, aberrant behavior.

> Rule of thumb: Don't allow a sick buyer to make you ill. If someone acts in a disturbed manner, they usually are. Cut your losses and walk away.

What to do if you don't get the business

Even with this methodical approach of relationship building, conceptual agreement, proposal as summation, choice of "yeses," and planned follow up, sometimes you don't get the business. As someone once said, that's not a failure, only the start of a new opportunity.

First, find out the only important piece of information for the moment: *WHY?* You can't do anything effectively until you learn the reason for your non-acceptance. The causes usually range among:

1. A legitimate, competing proposal was accepted.

2. Your proposal was flawed in some way.

3. Despite value, you were deemed as too expensive.

4. The project was canceled or postponed.

5. The prospect has decided to proceed using internal resources.

6. You weren't dealing with the true buyer.

Action Items

7. There was an internal upheaval or reorganization.

8. Someone talked the buyer out of using you (you were a threat).

9. Poor profitability has put a freeze on all expenditures.

10. The situation unexpectedly improved or the problem disappeared.

11. Unexpected profits have diminished the problem's priority.

12. A scandal occurs in the company (harassment, embezzlement, etc.).

13. The organization is sold, merges, or divests.

14. New technology eliminates the problem or opportunity.

15. Some combination of the above.

Believe it or not, I've heard every one of these reasons and excuses after submitting a proposal over 27 years as a consultant. The main reason to find out what the cause of your rejection was is that you want to be able to correct anything that was in your power to do so. Reasons #2, 3, and 6 are the ones to learn from. You can correct your mistakes or omissions in future proposals (it's too late for this one). The others are simply part of the fates and futures that await all consultants, and there's no use getting upset about them.

However, no matter what the cause, there are some actions that I advise you take whenever a proposal has formally been rejected.

We all get rejected. It comes with the turf. For those of you newer to the profession, let me apprise you right here: You will continually be rejected. For those of you who, like me, have been around long enough to know this, let us take a few seconds to commiserate.

All right, time's up.

Rejection needn't be the final bell. All that it signifies is that at that particular point, for that particular buyer, under those particular conditions, there wasn't sufficient perceived value. You've lost the battle, but the war is far from over. The good news is that you've met the buyer, established enough of a relationship to have been able to submit a proposal, and you know where the buyer lives. This is all the ammunition you'll need to begin mounting your counteroffensive.

Here are the six steps to take to turn short-term rejection into long-term business:

First, never walk away angry. The failure to consummate a business deal isn't the buyer's fault or your fault. It's not about fault, it's about *cause*. Take your setback gracefully, thank the buyer for all of the support and interest he or she has demonstrated along the way and, if another resource was chosen, say something nice about them and assure the buyer that you believe they'll do a fine job. Now, this is *very important*: Ask permission to stay in touch. This vague and simple request is rarely denied, but its acceptance by the buyer creates a legitimacy to the steps below. It's the difference between structured follow up and incessant hounding.

> You *have* been successful at creating a buyer-level relationship. Don't allow that to be rejected along with the proposal, or you really will have failed.

Second, ask for the cause of your not being chosen. Tell the buyer that we all learn best with honest feedback, and in the spirit of improving your approaches and helping other clients better in the future, ask what you could have done better, included, omitted, or changed. Don't settle for generic pap. ("It was close—it could have just as easily been you who was selected." Yeah, but it wasn't.) Ask for specific areas to work on and, no matter what you think of the advice, demonstrably take notes (if you're on the phone, say something like, "Just a second, I want to make a note of that."). Use the 15-point list above if you want to stimulate the conversation. Remember that there can be multiple causes.

Third, make an open offer to be of informal assistance if the buyer needs anything during the project (e.g., another opinion, a sounding board, etc.). At that juncture, provide your card and brochure or media kit *again*, for future reference (these are often discarded after a consultant hasn't made the cut).

Fourth, mail something—virtually anything of some value—to the buyer 30 days later, and bimonthly thereafter. Let the buyer know that there are no hard feelings, and that you have his or her interests in mind on a regular basis. Don't attempt to resurface the project you lost out on; simply send articles and materials that are relevant for the buyer's position, company, and/or industry.

Fifth, call the buyer about 90–120 days after your rejection, and ask any one of, or all of, the following questions: Has the material you've been sending been appropriate? Should you alter the content in any fashion? How has the project progressed? (If it's gone very well, indicate that

Action Items

you're delighted; if it's gone poorly, provide genuine empathy.) Tell the buyer that you'll be in the neighborhood on three different dates, and ask if you might have lunch or briefly meet on any of the three that are convenient.

Sixth, if you can meet with the buyer "while you're in the neighborhood," do so. During that meeting, develop a conversation about the current concerns and needs of the organization. Bring the buyer up to date on anything you've been doing *that's relevant to the buyer's needs.* If you're unable to arrange such a meeting, then go back to the third step above over the phone, and continue in the sequence.

If you're disciplined and unselfishly helpful, eventually the buyer will either agree to see you again, or request that you submit a proposal on some issue that has arisen. I've been called continually through the years by people who originally did not "click" with me, or who did a small amount of business in an unrelated area, merely because I've kept in touch. Consistency is everything. Don't contact people only when you want something, or when it's convenient for you. Establish regular helping patterns. You've already done the hard part in establishing the relationship to begin with.

It's always interested me that consultants follow-up *too much* on long shots, such as tentative leads and vague inquiries, and *not enough* on high potential future business, such as buyers who requested a proposal at some point.

The legendary coach Vince Lombardi said once that his teams had never lost a football game, although occasionally they had run out of time before they could win it. You have all the time in the world if you're consistent, professional, low key, and oriented toward a helping relationship.

Related to this general process is the delicate situation of key contacts and even buyers who are downsized, retire early, transferred to non-buying positions, and are the victims of innumerable other unpleasant fates. My advice is to continue to treat everyone with respect and support. Don't remove people from your mail list under any circumstances other than their specific request to do so. When you show someone that your respect and relationship was for the *person*, not the position or the ability to buy something from you, you create enduring ties. In many cases, that out-of-work individual comes roaring back in a powerful new position, and guess whom they'll feel comfortable inviting in to assist them in their new challenges?

I have received major pieces of business from working with downsized executives, providing *pro bono* work, taking the trouble to trace people who have abruptly left their companies and reestablish communication, and keeping in contact with people who seemed to have given me the cold shoulder. While I never accept rudeness, I will accept the fact that I might not have been the buyer's cup of tea at a particular juncture in our relationship.

That means, of course, that things can only improve.

Quick Start: Place the follow-up sequence for rejected proposals into your contact management or project management system, and include it in your weekly discipline through these prompts and reminders.

Summary of Chapter 5:

- Follow up must be planned and confirmed in advance.

- Follow up should be a continuation of the relationship, not a restart.

- Never discuss fees; discuss value.

- There are non-responsive buyers who can't be changed. Don't go crazy.

- Learn from those situations in which you are unsuccessful.

- Try not to burn your bridges.

Self-Assessment Questions:

1. How often do you confirm a follow-up when submitting the proposal?

2. What percentage of your proposals are accepted without having to renegotiate or make another appearance?

3. What percentage of your proposals are accepted after making adjustments or additional appearances?

4. How often do you feel compelled to lower your fees to gain acceptance?

5. Have you ever been able to obtain business from a buyer who didn't accept a prior proposal?

Action Items

Chapter Six

All the Other Stuff

I've chosen to take all of the peripheral and "other stuff" and place it in one chapter near the conclusion. That's not to say that this stuff isn't important. Portions of it might apply to some of you more than others, most of it will be situational for all of you, but all of it ought to be mastered if you're to develop project-winning proposals and enduring client relationships.

The "other stuff" includes these areas:

- Avoiding contracts, lawyers, and purchasing departments.

- What to do about RFPs.[1]

- When to negotiate further and when not to.

- Expanding current projects through additional proposals.

- Keeping it simple: When to violate my advice.

Avoiding contracts, lawyers, and purchasing departments

We've established that, in general, the more time it takes to read, review, discuss, process, and sign a proposal, the more opportunity exists for something to go wrong. A corollary of that theorem is that the more people involved, the more chance that someone, somewhere, will say "no."

A decision maker's "yes" needs no further reinforcement. That's a done deal in most cases. Therefore, the more the decision maker's "yes" is stamped, processed, reviewed, analyzed, and bureaucratized, the more likely it is that some stamper, processor, reviewer, analyst, and/or bureaucrat will find some obscure, tortured reason to suggest a "no." In any sane world, that means that you want to keep the proposal out of the hands of the chief naysayers: lawyers, financial analysts, and purchasing agents.

Lawyers

First understand that lawyers are employed to give the most conservative possible advice that they are able to muster. Their ideal universe comprises risk-free worlds. If the object is never to be sued, then the point is never to do anything that might expose one to lawsuit. The ultimate extrapolation of that position is to eliminate customers and suppliers, which would, after all, remove all such risk. Short of that, corporate attorneys will always, without fail, advocate the safest course despite low benefit. In other words, minimum payback is justified by the near-absence of any attendant risk.[2]

There are three preventive actions that tend to keep a proposal away from the legal department:

1. *Do not* use a lawyer yourself to create the proposal. I was contacted once by one of my mentorees who needed feedback on a proposal she was creating. She called and said, "I'm sitting here with my lawyer drawing up the contract, and I need to ask you something." I responded, "Can you get out of there as quickly as possible and call me when you're alone?"

If you use an attorney to create a proposal, you will manufacture a legal document, complete with "parties of the second part who shall hold parties of the first part harmless . . ." You don't need a lawyer. You are not protecting your estate, nor buying property. You are merely formalizing an agreement with an economic buyer *with whom you already have both a relationship and an agreement in principle.* Use the templates in the prior chapters and the resources in the appendix to create your own summary agreements: your proposal.

2. *Do not* create a proposal that sounds like or appears to be a contract. The only thing worse than using a lawyer to create a proposal is trying to create a quasi-contract yourself. Keep your verbiage conversational. Refer back to

---

[1] Requests for proposals, used extensively by the government, often by non-profits, and occasionally by private sector organizations.

[2] This is why you see signs at train stations that say "Do not stand on tracks when train is approaching," and stickers on floodlights that state, "Do not stare into lighted bulb. Doing so may cause eye damage."

Action Items

past points of agreement and cohesion. Do not use boiler-plate paragraphs to try to make the document appear to be more formal. This is yet another reason why effective proposals are *brief, conversational, and based on prior agreements.*

3. *Do* remind your buyer prior to submitting the proposal that you will create a summary of your agreement (the proposal) that will constitute the working agreement between the two of you. Feel free to state directly that you are comfortable with the two of you moving forward, that a "handshake" is good enough to begin the process, and that there is no need to pass the agreement through lawyers at either end *in your experience with other clients.* Most buyers will respond, "That's the last thing I want to do around here," and you'll be home free. At the very least, you're reminding them that there's no need to involve the legal department.

> Attorneys are very good at what they do, and what they do is minimize risk. The aspect of an outsider coming into the organization to poke around and conduct studies has "risk" written all over it.

If your relationship with a true buyer isn't good enough to begin a project—on either side—with a verbal handshake, then no amount of legal help is going to improve that condition. You haven't developed the relationship you need to begin with, and further legal review will continue to weaken it.

Contracts

Some organizations will have standardized contracts that they require be signed. The documents can be lengthy, and the boilerplate often contains some unpleasant surprises. For example, my proposals always stipulate that a project is non-cancelable, but many contracts guarantee the client the ability to cancel a project unilaterally without *cause and without penalty* with a 30-day notification. Other contracts will demand esoterica that can significantly slow down acceptance. One client contract demanded that I produce a "license to do business" which, though readily available in the client's state of incorporation, was un-

known in mine. It took two weeks to educate the contract people that such a document could not be produced.[3]

Contracts will always delay a project's approval, and they will sometimes pose serious drawbacks to the consultant (limits on expenditures, highly detailed reporting, personal and/or company financial statements, etc.). The main reason is that contracts are drawn up to include *all* possible vendors and suppliers of services, so the people delivering computers, contractors pouring cement, and consultants running focus groups are all lumped together as "vendors."

Here's how to avoid trouble:

1. Ask the buyer if there is a contract office or provision for your services, or if the two of you can proceed on the basis of a mutually-acceptable proposal from you. If there is a contract provision, ask the buyer if the two of you can reach agreement outside of that system since it rarely pertains to your kind of work. A significant-level buyer usually has the authority to make his or her own agreements.

2. If contracts are unavoidable, read them carefully (here's where you can use *your* lawyer) and then *negotiate any unacceptable points with the buyer, not the contracting agent.* That is, recruit the buyer as your negotiator internally. Tell the buyer that the unilateral cancellation clause is unacceptable and needs to be waived (or extended to 60 days).

3. Pick your fights, and don't die on the wrong hill. There is nothing wrong with providing financial information or signing nondisclosure agreements. Detailed receipts for all expenses and a 60-day reimbursement arrangement might be annoying but acceptable. But a provision that states that you cannot run internal meetings without a representative of human resources present will compromise your intent to assure confidentiality when conducting interviews. Determine what's truly unacceptable and then stand your ground.

4. Ask the buyer if you can begin on the initial aspects of the project while the contract is being finalized so that key time frames are not jeopardized. Make it clear that you are doing this as a favor to the buyer, and that you expect to get paid for your work if, in the worst case, the contract isn't approved. Put that all in writing. Often, the *fait accompli* approach works very well. I've seen contracts fi-

---

[3] However, there are some contract provisions that you can anticipate and you have to satisfy. Some organizations, for instance, demand that consultants carry errors and omissions (malpractice) insurance or they will not approve a project.

Action Items

nally signed after virtually all of the work has been done and payments made.

5. Segment the proposal. In many cases, contracts are required only in excess of certain thresholds. If that threshold is, say, $50,000, suggest to the buyer that you provide two separate proposals, phase I and phase II, each for $25,000, submitted concurrently or 30 days apart. I know it sounds obvious, but it almost always works.[4]

6. Finally, as suggested in earlier chapters, always try to get paid in advance. That way, in the worst case—an onerous contract in which a cancellation clause is actually invoked—you already have your money. If you're paid in advance and a project in canceled, do you return the excess? That's your decision. My position is this: I was paid in accordance with the contract and performed in accordance with the contract. Cancellation was not about the quality of my work, but about other organizational issues. I'm happy to begin work again at any time in the next 12 months without penalty to the client. But I ain't returning the money. (Many companies have purchasing policies that state all discounts offered MUST be accepted, hence, a 10% discount for full payment in advance will often sail through the process.)

> Don't sign a contract merely to begin
> the project and start collecting your
> fees. There are always hidden
> surprises, none in your favor. If you
> can't avoid them, negotiate; if you
> can't negotiate, get paid early;
> if you can't get paid early,
> think carefully about your
> downside risk before you sign.

I've seen many colleagues burned by contracts that eroded their margins to the point of a loss on the project, delayed payments until the money was significantly discounted, or ended projects prior to just compensation. Your sequence should be: avoid if possible, negotiate if allowable, counterpunch if necessary.

---

[4] I have had executives ask me for four concurrent invoices of $24,900 each, for example. In a $100,000 contract with a $25,000 contract limit, I gladly waive the $400 I'll be short!

Purchasing Agents

Purchasing departments are ideally organized to obtain the best deals on pens, desks, vehicles, new roofs, and parking lot lines. They are the worst possible source to evaluate or approve consulting help.

Even worse, you usually have no opportunity to establish a relationship with "purchasing," that mysterious entity known only by its phone extensions. The function epitomizes the nameless, faceless bureaucracy.

Here's how to avoid this limbo:

1. Try to co-opt the process by explaining to the buyer that your type of services generally are not understood by purchasing. Can you and the buyer merely reach agreement between the two of you?

2. If purchasing is a required stop, then can the buyer personally intervene to expedite the proposal? Usually, a significant-level buyer will have a colleague or contact who can short-cut the process. Remind the buyer that time is of the essence.

3. Find out if there is someone in purchasing who is a key contact for consulting proposals. Give that person a call. I've found that a proactive, personal strike will often grease the skids. Ask that person *what you can do for them* to make the transaction as easy as possible. Offer to stop in or to provide additional information by phone. Make sure they have your number (or e-mail address) in case they have questions. *You want purchasing to call you, not to exchange conventional letters.*

4. In the event of excessive delays or an impasse, go to the buyer and explain that you're at a go/no go point, and that further delay or demands will be a deal breaker. A general manager once shook my hand on a project and told me that purchasing would simply implement the contract. The next week, the purchasing agent opened up with a salvo that included the fact that she was going to renegotiate the fee.

ME: "But the general manager and I agree on the entire project, including the fee."

HER: "He does not know how to negotiate with vendors. I will do that with you."

ME: "I am not a vendor. I'm a consultant, and this is how I charge for my work."

HER: "You're a vendor as far as I'm concerned, and we negotiate this fee downward to a *per diem* arrangement, or we have no project."

ME: "Good-bye."

Action Items

I called the general manager and told him we had a problem that would probably break the deal. His response was classic: "Do you need more money?" he ingenuously asked. (I thought about that for a few moments.) When I explained the problem, he said, "I've heard that she acts that way. I'll take care of it."

The purchasing agent was fired. There was a history, and I was the final straw. Did I feel badly about it? Not at all. Did the project succeed? You bet.

> Don't allow yourself to be tossed about by the purchasing fates. Try to avoid that course. If it can't be avoided, try to forge a relationship with a navigator.

Of course, never, ever treat a purchasing agent as the buyer. They are implementers of contracts only, and usually not implementers of yours.

What to do about RFPs

Requests for proposals are used extensively by government agencies. In many cases, the law requires that they do so to ensure a fair purchasing process. Unfortunately, when the buying process for services is deconstructed into component parts, the quality and intellectual heft of the provider—which is the entire point of hiring a consultant to begin with—is left in the dust in favor of cost of materials, cost of travel, number of days required, subcontracting costs, and all the other measurable tasks that afford employment for so many bureaucrats.

It's a wonderfully precise, objective, visible system. The only problem is that it virtually never ensures the best quality of consulting help (and, in my observation, doesn't even ensure the best quality plumber, roofer, or pencil supplier, but that's another story).

Many nonprofits also use RFPs to demonstrate "fairness" and avoid charges of favoritism by executive and board members, and some for-profits use them as well. One huge problem with them is the expense associated with completing them. They are usually lengthy documents, requiring a great deal of calculation, project speculation, and information gathering to complete, and they are almost always required in multiples of four, six, eight, or whatever. It seems that bureaucrats don't own a copy machines.

Moreover, they effectively preclude any kind of relationship with a buyer if the rules are precisely followed. They are deliberately faceless and nameless, and the sole contact provided is usually a purchasing agent. You have no idea who the competition is in most cases, and often the buyer is not required to select the lowest bid (which is good) but they almost always will (which is bad). The reviewers, in my experience, are invariably uneducated in the role and use of consultants, and inevitably track the wrong criteria (e.g., how many days are required as opposed to what kind of results are generated).

RFPs assume a problem (we are growing faster than we can manage), a solution (we need a training program on retaining good people), and an input-oriented measurement (success will be represented by 90% of frontline managers undergoing the training). Because they are drawn up by people closest to the problem, they consistently ignore internal causes for those problems.

Finally, payment terms are inflexible, never favorable to the consultant, and the clients are notorious for either missing payment dates or making additional demands before paying because some detail or other was presumably not fully documented. These contracts not only all have draconian cancellation clauses, but there are also penalty provisions in many in case you don't meet a deadline or hit a bull's eye.

> RFPs are expensive to complete, use all the wrong criteria for selection, preclude a relationship, are reviewed by people who don't understand consulting, and are completely structured with bias against the provider. Other than that, they're great.

Here are some suggestions on how to deal with RFPs:

1. Ignore them. They are enormously costly in terms of both time and energy and the chances of success are remote. Don't waste your time. There are innumerable other opportunities out there which present better odds and higher quality relationships.

2. Try to become a sole-source provider, thereby circumventing the need to appear on GSA[5] and similar lists. That

---

[5] General Services Administration, which provides lists of approved resources who may be sent RFPs on the federal level. There are similar state agencies.

Action Items

means that if you can demonstrate to a buying authority that you are unique in the product or service you provide, you may be dealt with directly and competitive bidding is not required. I've completed many government jobs in which the buyer said to me from the outset, "Let's see how we can position you as a sole-source provider." A unique expertise, copyrighted program, patented model, distinctive business book, and other devices can qualify you. Some jurisdictions are more accommodating than others.

3. Work the system to its fullest extent. Every RFP includes a face-to-face meeting for vendors which provides additional information, and is conducted by an agency representative (often the purchasing agent). Although this involves travel to the site (there is rarely more than one meeting, of course), you will be able to ask questions, scope out your serious competition (who will also be in the room), and develop a small relationship with at least the person present.

4. Try to bend the system by meeting the buyer or the key recommenders. This is difficult, but not impossible. You may say that your company's policy is to meet such people prior to submitting a bid, or that you can't make the general information meeting and you'd like to know if there is any way to meet at another time. If you already know some of the people involved (after all, someone had to send you the RFP to begin with) then try to talk to them, even if by phone.

5. Sometimes an effective relationship with a buyer will produce an RFP that *only* you can fill. The RFP will specify your geography, or your approach, or some traits that are impossible to find in anyone else in that combination.

6. *Always* provide more than only the RFP response. Complete the RFP fully, and in detail, but then provide some options not called for but that, in your judgment, would enhance the project. There are no rules against providing more than is demanded. and I've known firms that secured business through complying with the specifications, thereby gaining entry to the competition, but then added creative options which gained the inside track for them. In the worst case, the options will be ignored or you'll be penalized by a super-punctilious bureaucrat; in the best case, you'll be distinctive.

Rule of thumb: If you're completing more than two RFPs a quarter, and you're not a specialist in government operations, you're spending far too much time on them.

When to negotiate further and when not to

Sometimes a proposal will stall and, like an airplane in a vertical position in which it was never intended to fly, you can either crash to the ground or restart the engine.

Some prospects will have financial problems, despite your choice of options. That usually means that your value is not seen as sufficient to justify even your lowest fee. Other prospects will have legitimate concerns over implementation or methodology, for example, the data gathering seems far too intrusive, or there isn't enough skills transfer to their own people.

My rule is to always negotiate on value, and to never negotiate solely on fee. In other words, if the prospect wants the fee reduced, then you must remove commensurate value (I can reduce the fee by 10% if we examine the domestic sales force but not the international sales force) or add value for yourself (I can reduce the fee by 10% if you pay the entire fee upon signing, thereby giving me use of my money and reducing administrative costs).

If you negotiate fee and not value, then the prospect has two main questions: How much lower can you go? How can I trust someone who padded their proposal by that much? Neither of these questions are conducive to building long-term trust and enduring relationships.

> If you are negotiating over fee and not value, you have lost control of the discussion. Stop doing that.

Here are some post-proposal objections and suggestions for when and how to negotiate from there. Remember, the prospect has reviewed your proposal, and is on the fence. He or she wouldn't have called you to continue the discussion if there were no interest.[6]

Objection: The timing isn't comfortable. We're not ready to move ahead as boldly as you suggest. We're concerned about disrupting the organization and creating more problems than we solve.

Response: That's a common and legitimate reservation. However, the timing will never be perfect. If we do nothing at all right now, what will be the trend of the problem?

---

[6] You might want to use this section for reference whenever a prospect replies, "We're just not sure."

Action Items

It will probably get worse, requiring even *more* extensive intervention when it becomes absolutely intolerable. Why don't we attack it now, but in phases? Where are you most comfortable beginning? I'll start there in the next week and we'll see how it goes.

Objection: I've gotten push-back from some colleagues (and/or people in my own division) that this will not be embraced and will be seen as a threat to people. I don't want to impose something on the staff.

Response: Let's keep in mind that, while we'd love to have everyone on board, the objective here is to improve this condition. People respond best to their leaders' example. Why don't we assemble your direct reports (or leadership team) and we'll specify what everyone's role is in making this a success? I'll be happy to meet one-on-one with anyone who has problems or needs some coaching. If you and your people set the tone, others will follow.

Objection: There is a strong feeling here that we can do this internally.

Response: That's probably true. But let me ask you something. If that's the case, why hasn't it been done thus far, and what guarantees do you have that it will be done according to the time frames that you and I have agreed are essential? Just because it can be done internally doesn't mean that it should be or will be. Besides, I can make a case that it will be far more expensive if done internally, once you add up salaries, time off the regular job, internal disruption, and your own need to supervise the project and act as referee between departments. You are also going to lose a high degree of objectivity.

Objection: Any way we look at it, it's just too expensive. Can we get the price down?

Response: Possibly, but we'd of course have to remove some of the planned work and commensurate benefits. For example, do you want to run the survey only internally, and not include customers . . .

Objection: We like it but we have a severe budget constraint. Here's our offer to you: Can you do the project for X% of your stated fee?

Response: Of course not. Could you sell your products at X% and still meet your shareholders' goals? I've enjoyed being able to work with you thus far. Please call me if conditions change and you can make the investment required.

Note that in all cases, I've tried to avoid an adversarial relationship by agreeing with the buyer's point, then countering with an argument in the buyer's favor. I've never said, "You're wrong and I'm right," merely that we're both right and I'd like you to look at this in another manner.

In the last case, you'll find that nothing succeeds like the honest, sincere willingness to walk away from business. I've been called back in that moment before I've even gathered my belongings at the table! You have to show you're serious about your craft. And if you do wind up walking away, you've saved yourself the futility of working on a project for less than your true worth.

Expanding current projects through additional proposals

If you have succeeded in establishing clear objectives for your project at the outset, then the dreaded "scope creep" will not occur. That is, the client will not be able to continually ask you for additional results and support services without realizing that they are beyond the scope of the existing agreement.[7]

The converse is that you can keep your eye out for additional opportunities for other projects while you're delivering the current one. If the projects are legitimate needs that will improve the client's condition, and you have the competency to address them, there is nothing but a win/win dynamic to this practice. After all, the buyer can always say "no."

There are two good ways to do this:

1. As you report to the buyer on current progress, suggest additional areas of focus *for the buyer* to be thinking about, since you've observed these in your travels. (An example: While visiting field sites to interview local staff for a sales productivity project, you notice that virtually no phone is ever answered by a human. All are left to ring and be picked up by voice mail, even though office people are clearly not too busy to answer them. You suggest to the buyer changing the system so that at least some customers can get a real person on certain lines.)

When you turn in progress reports or final reports, include a section titled something like "Peripheral Issues" or "Additional Observations." Make it clear that there were not in the context of your current project, but that it's ethically incumbent upon you to bring certain issues and opportunities to the attention of the buyer. Don't ask for the work. Merely bring up the need.

2. Reach out to other buyers. All organizations have scores of buyers accordingly to my definition (someone who can write a check for your services).

---

[7] Of course, if you choose to respond to every client request by agreeing to it on the basis that you're afraid to deal with the buyer as a peer, then you deserve what you'll get, which will be eroded margins and, ironically, a client who is never really happy.

Action Items

My advice is to view a few large accounts not as huge clients, but as multiple buying sites. After all, if you're doing business with a department or division of a huge company, the chances are strong that other parts of that company operate as if they are independent businesses. In some cases (e.g., GE's locomotive and light bulb businesses) they really are. However, in most cases they act as if they are.

While you're implementing a project, you should be on the alert for additional relationships that can be developed. I'm not talking about blatant internal marketing, but rather about intelligently providing value-added for other economic buyers you encounter while delivering your existing project. For example, I recently designed a communications strategy for a global company. My buyer was an executive charged by the CEO to create and implement such a strategy. In the course of a nine-month implementation, three other buyer relationships developed.

First, a senior vice president responsible for improving all corporate meetings became involved with my original project as a participant, and asked my opinion of using an overall communications strategy to improve officer meetings. I provided her with my ideas, met with her three times at her office, and ultimately suggested a survey project which would embrace the participants themselves in design suggestions. She accepted and I concurrently completed that project while still implementing the original one that had brought us together. In conducting those surveys and interviews, I developed a list of organizational issues that I've suggested she present to the CEO for possible action. If he determines any require response, then I may be involved in the resolution of those.

Second, while taking the original project to international sites, I talked to the executive vice president of international operations, who had also been a participant in my first project, to gain his insights on overseas communications needs. He raised some organizational and political issues which were causing him problems. I suggested that after I finished my international trips I compile a list of critical issues that the groups raised and provide my own interpretation of those issues, so that he might have them as an additional input in his decision-making process. He readily agreed, and I presented that to him the next year, when he asked me to become formally involved.

Finally, the general counsel, after being interviewed by me for the communications strategies, asked if I'd submit a proposal to facilitate a legal retreat. I did, but he ultimately chose another resource. However, we remain friends, and I'm confident he'll ask me to bid on future projects. You don't win them all, but you don't win any if you're not asked.

During the course of my work at that firm, I've met virtually all senior officers, interviewed them and/or had them in one of my workshops, and seen many on several occasions. I consistently try to provide value to them where possible in the course of their own responsibilities. I want them to think of me as a resource when something formal is required. Each new buyer receives a separate proposal based upon the outcomes desired for his or her project.

> Once you've been hired with the imprimatur of a key buyer, use that credibility to meet and develop relationships with other potential buyers in the course of your project. Those opportunities are constantly present.

It's always best to have a diverse array of clients. This provides for maximum learning and growth, as well as financial protection. However, if you come upon times when you have only a few large clients, then view them as multiple buying sites, and create a proactive strategy to develop relationships with as many potential buyers as possible. Provide value for free, be accessible, and listen carefully. You're already credible, since you've been hired elsewhere in the organization, and you've already been educated about the overall culture.

Preserving your independent contractor status

Some words of caution, important for newcomers, but also for some veterans: If you derive almost all of your income from a single client, the IRS can make a case that you are an employee and not an independent contractor. Even if the IRS is unreasonable, the fight can cost you a small fortune and the client might be scared off (since it means withholding taxes, social security, etc.). Your ability to make certain deductions and spend pretax income will be jeopardized. I've seen consultants, instructional designers, trainers, and many others fall into this trap because they take on a huge piece of work and forsake all others.

Check with your lawyer and your financial adviser if your revenues are mainly restricted to a single source. Since many employers have attempted to use this approach to avoid the expense of full-time payrolls, the issue is a major one with the IRS that you may be inadvertently trapped within.

Action Items

Keeping it simple:
When to violate my advice

While I have strong ideas about these matters, they are supported by an ocean of flexibility. In other words, I don't demand that a buyer go through all of my steps if the buyer says, "Let's do it." I never oversell, over-orchestrate, or over-manage.

I've provided examples in the appendix of proposals that adhere to all of my steps and others that simply match some of my steps. I've also provided letters of agreement and letters of confirmation that short-cut the process when I've achieved a very early buying signal. Remember my maxim: The longer it takes, the more that can go wrong.[8]

Please take my advice to improve *your* condition. But do so intelligently. You might embrace my complete approach to relationships and proposal building; you might simply focus on a few aspects, such as obtaining clear and measurable objectives; or you may take merely bits and pieces, such as how to handle certain objections.

Violate my advice whenever you feel that doing so will increase your chances of getting the proposal accepted. I won't take it personally. All I suggest is that, if you're not as successful in this profession as you'd like to be, that there is a wealth of techniques and approaches in this book that could make the difference for you. Find out where you're weak, where you go wrong, where the client throws you off track, and use this resource to improve your business.

That's my proposal. I hope you'll accept. It's not about my approaches, it's about your results.

Quick Start: Find three ideas in this book that will improve your proposal "hit rate" and start using them tomorrow.

Summary of Chapter 6:

• The client's lawyers may be nice people, but I've never known one who improved a consultant's proposal.

• Try to avoid or minimize the use of formal client contracts.

• If you must sign a client's contract, read the thing before doing so. The fine print might cause you severe indigestion when you least expect it.

• Use your relationship with the buyer to break bureaucratic impasses.

• RFPs are almost always a poor investment of your time. If you do choose to respond to them, stack the deck in your favor.

• There is nothing wrong with negotiating over a proposal, so long as it's about value and not about fees.

• There is nothing illegal or unethical about investigating additional business while implementing existing business. This is technically known as "intelligent marketing."

• Stay flexible. Don't dogmatically follow any single path. Not even if I've recommended it!

Self-Assessment Questions:

1. What percentage of the time do you conclude business with the buyer rather than with purchasing agents, lawyers, or other intermediaries?

2. Do you provide the proposal every time, or do you allow the client to provide a contract without resistance?

3. Have you ever reached agreement with a buyer only to have the project vetoed by a lower-level intermediary?

4. Do you actively seek additional business within existing clients by bringing to their attention other problems and opportunities you've discovered?

5. Are you willing to alter your approach to get business given the uniqueness of any given prospect?

---

[8] Have you ever tried to purchase any high-tech gizmo where the technical guru continues to sell you on its merits and advantages long after you've said, "I'll take it"? These are very confused people.

Action Items

Chapter Seven

Questions from Readers

Since the original publication of this book in 1999, I've been the quite pleasantly surprised recipient of weekly questions from readers, audience members, and participants in my Mentor Program about all aspects of proposals. I've selected the most frequent and/or most intriguing of those questions and reproduced them here with my responses and reactions. By addressing them here I'm able to provide succinct replies to specific concerns, rather than write another ten chapters on aspects that might not apply or appeal to every reader.

Q. Do I always need a proposal? What about those situations where I've done work with the client before and I'm comfortable proceeding with a handshake?

A. You might not need a proposal as complete as detailed in this book, but you do need something because of what I call "the beer truck syndrome." That is: What happens if your buyer gets hit by a beer truck? You must have something in writing to confirm the conceptual agreement, fees, and terms, at least. I'd suggest, at a minimum, a "letter of agreement" which outlines all pertinent understandings and agreement and which is in hard copy in your files and your buyer's. Ideally, I'd like to see it signed.

Q. I continually confuse objectives and value. Can you provide me with a quick definition and differentiation?

A. An *objective* is a business outcome desired by the buyer from the project. An example would be increased retention of key employees, or more effective management teamwork. A *measure* (or metric) is an indicator of progress toward those objectives and successful attainment of them. An example for each of the objectives above would be "decrease in new hires who leave within the first 12 months of employment" and "senior managers voluntarily share resources without the need for mediation by a superior." *Value* is the worth of the objectives to the organization and the buyer. Continuing our example: The value might be a savings of $45,000 for each person additionally retained (representing the costs of a new replacement, recruiting, training, etc.) and a management team focused on customer need (and therefore building business) rather than protecting turf. Another example: A 2% sales increase might be an objective, the measure is

the monthly sales report, and the value is $600,000 annually.

Q. Shouldn't I protect myself and minimize liability by adding "boilerplate" sections that include legal provisions, such as how disputes will be handled, in what state, and in what manner?

A. Once you include legal language, your buyer really has no options but to forward the proposal to his or her legal department. That will immediately result in two unpleasantries: First, the client's lawyers will change the language to gain a more favorable position. Second, there will be an inevitable and lengthy delay, endangering your entire project. I've also found that no amount of legal language will protect you from someone intent on suing you, and that an outstanding client relationship is the absolute best protection against this. In summary: Adding the boilerplate provides more downside risk than it does long-term protection.

Q. I'm on very good terms with a buyer who must take my proposal to a key executive for buy-off. Should I send a copy to this executive whom I've never met, or simply trust my contact?

A. Bad news, but your contact isn't a buyer. Buyer's can *buy*–sign a check. They don't need buy-off from anyone else. Consequently, I'd try to meet that real buyer before you even submit the proposal, because you don't have conceptual agreement with a buyer, but rather only with a gatekeeper. You've probably wasted too much time already dealing with your current contact.

Q. The client has responded with a contract of their own, and they mandate that it be signed as a condition of doing work. The terms are different from what I proposed, e.g., they can cancel with ten days' notice at no penalty. How do I handle this?

A. Don't try to argue with the purchasing department or the legal people. Instead, go to your buyer and ask for some relief. In other words, you're happy to sign the client contract IF some of your interests can be preserved. For example, a ten-day cancellation is unduly onerous, and you prefer that it be either removed or extended to 60

Action Items

days. If you have the proper relationship with your buyer and the buyer truly needs the work done, an accommodation will almost always be made.

Q. What happens when I've received all payments due and the client keeps postponing the balance of my work? What do I owe the client and for how long?

A. Since the client is postponing, you don't owe anything other than to complete the project at a mutually-agreeable time. But bear in mind that too long a delay could imperil success (e.g., data is out of date, opportunity has been lost, people are no longer available). Normally, I recommend that you try to reschedule as quickly as possible but apprise the client that the project may become untenable if the delay is too long. In such case, the project may need to be restructured—at an additional fee—or abandoned, with you keeping the fee already paid. This is why I always recommend trying to get paid in advance or at least in a brief time span after commencement. And it's why it's mandatory to stipulate that the project is non-cancelable once commenced. Keep in mind that it's not your job to insist on completion if your client, for good reasons or bad, isn't amenable to continuing. And it is perfectly ethical and acceptable to retain the fees paid since your time has been committed and you've acted in good faith.

Q. I've just been told that an annoying back problem is worse than I imagined and I'll need surgery that will keep me incapacitated for six weeks or more. I was due to begin a major project within that period. What are my options with the client?

A. You have three primary options for the clients: First, you can explain the situation and determine whether the client is willing to wait. Second, you can ask the client if you can provide replacements (assuming you can acquire them) to perform the work. Third, you can offer to refund whatever fees you have been paid. You're best bet is to allow the client to decide which method is most beneficial.

Q. I know you say that a proposal shouldn't be a negotiating document, but I've had prospects who put tremendous pressure on me by saying, "We love what you've offered, and if you can reduce the fee by 20% we can shake hands and begin tomorrow." Should I anticipate this by padding the fee, or just bite the bullet and accept a lower margin?

A. Neither. I'll give you the preventive and contingent actions. The preventive is to offer options in every proposal (not stages or phases, but increasingly valuable alternatives). By doing so, you're changing the psychology from "Should I do this or not?" to "Which of these is the best option for me?" For example, one option may be a sales

audit, training design, and implementation. A second, however, may be to also transfer the capability to the client to improve the process every two years or so. And a third may be to first begin with a benchmarking study of other organizations so that a "world class" improvement process can be implemented. Any of the alternatives will work, but each successive one offers increasing value (and requires an increasing fee). The contingent action, if you haven't offered options, is to say, "I'll try to reduce the fee if you tell me what value to remove." In other words, perhaps you'll have to leave out the international people or cancel the six-month follow-up. Buyers love to reduce fee, but they hate to remove value. If you reduce fee without removing value you've indicated that continuing pressure will probably result in lower and lower fees, and you've laid the groundwork for your own poverty. (If you have given options and the buyer says, "We love option 3 but the fee is too high," then reply, "That's why there's an option 2.")

Q. Can I anticipate and build expenses into the proposal, thereby eliminating monthly billing and having the money to use in advance?

A. Yes, of course. There are two ways to do this, assuming you can obtain fairly accurate estimates and there isn't much chance of the client or you deciding on increased travel as the project progresses. First, you can separate the projected expenses and indicate an additional $7,500 (or whatever) in the proposal, demonstrating that by prepaying the expenses the client's costs are effectively capped in that area (because you will have to absorb any overage). The second method is to simply cite a fee *and indicate it is inclusive of expenses* which will often be quite appealing to the client. If your margins are high enough—and with my preferred value-based pricing they will be—then you're even protected against underestimating the expense.

Q. I've been told to put strict time limits in my proposals, e.g., "valid for 60 days from this date." Is that a good idea?

A. There's nothing wrong with doing that, but I'll tell you why I find it irrelevant. Since my proposals are based on conceptual agreement beforehand, I'm expecting a "go/no go" decision within 24 hours of its receipt. And I tell the buyer that I'll be calling within 24 hours after receipt if I don't hear from the buyer first. So the issue is moot about expiry dates as far as I'm concerned. Besides, if someone unearthed an old proposal and told you it could now be accepted, you'd nonetheless have the option of saying that you'd have to rewrite it because conditions had changed in the interim. Just because there is no expiry date doesn't mean it's infinitely acceptable.

Action Items

Q. Why don't you put credentials and background about your firm, yourself, your subcontractors right in the proposal document? We were taught to do that religiously in the large consulting firm I was with.

A. I find this unnecessary. At the point of proposal submission you should have a relationship with the buyer which has already established your credibility and, since it is with the buyer, there is no need to anticipate having to impress someone reading the proposal whom you haven't met. It's far better to keep the proposal short and crisp, so that the focus can be on results and ROI. You never know when ancillary material may just turn a buyer off, and it seldom helps with the sale. (Your subcontractors may all be young, or male, or you may have gone to a school which was an arch-rival of the buyer. Sales have been lost on more minor issues.)

Q. I understand the need for a trusting relationship, but how do you know when you've achieved it?

A. To me, trust means that two people have the honest-to-goodness belief that the other person has their best interests in mind. Consequently, I'll listen to feedback, critique, even opposition from someone I trust to have my best interests in mind, but I'll be skeptical of even praise, reward, and gifts from someone who I do not believe has my best interests in mind. You know you have trust when the other person shares personal beliefs and fears, when they listen to contrasting opinions, and when they respond to your questions without hedging or reservation. When the other person says, "I'm not sure yet," or "Well, what do you think," or "I'm not ready to discuss that," you don't have trust yet.

Q. What percentage of my proposals should I reasonably expect to close if I follow your process?

A. I hit about 80%—remember that I send out fewer proposals than most professionals because I wait until I obtain conceptual agreement—and I'd suggest that you ought to close at least two out of three with this format.

Q. What are the greatest causes of not closing a proposal even after appearing to do all the right things?

A. In other words, why will you still fail about a third of the time? Here are my "usual suspects":

- Wrong buyer: Despite it all, you haven't been talking to the economic buyer, and the real buyer turned it down.

- Lack of enough appealing options: You presented a "take it or leave it" and the buyer left it.

- Lack of conceptual agreement: You thought you heard it, but you never tested it and never verified it with the buyer before submitting the proposal.

- The unexpected: Sometimes a "deus ex machina" appears in the form of a new corporate policy, economic downturn, or other unexpected, traumatic event, and your once attractive value fades by comparison with new exigencies.

- Poor ROI: You can price a proposal far too high if the buyer isn't getting a good deal in the buyer's perception. In purely quantitative terms, I would think that a ten-to-one return would be a minimal expectation. In a qualitative framework, the buyer would need his or her conditions significantly and demonstrably improved (repute, stress alleviation, independence, etc.).

- Total focus on corporate goals: Behind every corporate goal is a personal goal of the buyer (e.g., better teamwork means less stress for the buyer, and higher sales means more bonus). You must ensure that the value is personally attractive, and not just organizationally significant. You're not selling to a corporate entity, you're selling to a human being, with all due emotions, foibles, and politics.

Q. A consultant told me that "proposal" is a poor term, denoting marriage, and that "contract" or "agreement" should be used. How important is that?

A. I've heard of trivial concerns, and that one takes the cake. I think your consultant friend is revealing his own weaknesses. I've seen "proposal" used in the highest and lowest circles without any repercussions. And once you talk about "contract" you're inviting the lawyers to weigh in. We all have more important things to worry about than how people view the word "proposal."

Q. When a client requests work outside of the proposal's objectives, is it best to write an addendum or a new proposal?

A. I don't think it matters much. I prefer a new proposal covering the new work, so as not to confuse the existing project and create a new fee schedule as appropriate. Also, this approach leaves the current project "intact" without a review by anyone of existing terms and conditions. You're smart to raise this issue, because the cause of the dreaded "scope creep" is the acceptance of additional work, outside of current objectives, within the existing project. That acceptance can erode profit margins dramatically. One of my consulting clients calls the unfortunate willingness to accept additional work for free "undocumented promises." In other words, the consultant promises to do things not documented in the existing agreement.

Q. Is it better to accept the client's measurement devices or to produce your own?

Action Items

A. All things being equal, it's better to produce your own for two reasons: First, you're providing extra value to the client by developing metrics which didn't exist before. Second, you're actually creating the criteria by which to measure your own success. Clients often have metrics in place, but very often they were designed for different conditions and different needs, and aren't ideal for your project. On the other hand, some measures, such as monthly sales reports or attrition statistics, are unarguably relevant.

Q. How can I indicate timing when I'm not certain that schedules will be upheld or key people will be available in a highly volatile environment?

A. I suggest you provide relative dates not calendar dates (e.g., "60 days after the first round of focus groups is complete" and not "by April 12th"). Also, indicate ranges ("between 60 and 90 days, depending on availability") and provide a disclaimer: "I'm assuming that you will provide information and people on dates specified, and that I will have open access to the manufacturing operation. If this changes, then the time frames will be pushed back commensurately."

Q. Would you begin work without a signed proposal if the client says to start?

A. Absolutely, *provided* that the buyer has said I can start, and that I verify that all terms and conditions are acceptable (in other words, my check is in the mail). I call this "pouring cement on the project" since, by starting immediately, it's that much more difficult for a last-minute reservation to undermine the project. I tell the buyer that I'm more than happy to begin on a "telephone handshake."

Q. What happens if I'm not paid as promised? What does "on acceptance" mean, anyway?

A. For me, it means that I receive my deposit or full payment when the buyer says he or she accepts my proposal, in writing or orally, even if the project doesn't begin for another month or more. If I'm to start immediately, I expect payment within a week. If I don't receive payment within a week, I follow-up with the buyer to ensure there are no snags. If there is no payment a week after that, and I'm not comfortable with the reason why, I will stop work, because that's not the basis of a partnership. (Similarly, when you are in the midst of a project and a scheduled payment doesn't arrive, use the same tactics. The only true leverage you have is preventing the value from being realized by halting the work.) I have never experienced a problem severe enough in this area to prompt me to stop working, however.

Q. After a project is completed, how long should I retain the proposal and related records? I'm starting to run out of physical space and computer space.

A. You can always transfer records to a storage medium and place them in a bank safety deposit box, but even these files will degrade over time. My policy is that two years is sufficient, providing the client is no longer active in any manner or in any area. Of course, retain all important contact information for your marketing needs.

Q. You've indicated there are nine basic steps in a good proposal. Is this a dynamic process, and do you anticipate adding to these as time goes on and you learn more?

A. I suppose that's always possible, since I'm constantly surprised at how stupid I was two weeks ago. But the current format is the result of over 25 years in consulting, and I've been using it for the last ten. I think the format comprehensively covers every single vital element, and efficiently eliminates the superfluous and superficial. I don't like to add bells and whistles for no reason, so I'm fairly confident that this is the template for the foreseeable future.

Action Items

Bonus!

101 Questions for Any Sales Situation You'll Ever Face

An overview

This material is intended to provide questions to ask in virtually any sales situation, thereby:

1. Maintaining a conversational and "non-sales" approach.

2. Keeping the other party talking in order to learn.

3. Avoiding "deselection" by volunteering very little yourself.

4. Finding the buyer, building a relationship, and closing business.

5. Accelerating the entire sales process.

The opposing page provides the opportunity for you to customize the questions to fit your particular type of sale, niche, specialty, or customer. I strongly advise that you personalize the generic questions so that they support your particular practice or business.

You might choose to take these on calls, to keep them by the phone, or to use them as the basis for printing out your own questions to keep in your briefcase or calendar. The copyright is intended to protect the work as it is presented, and to avoid resale or unethical use. However, you should feel free to incorporate the generic questions and the derivations that flow from them into your personal routine and support materials.

The questions are deliberately overlapping, and stop just short of duplicative. Essentially, you want to elicit the same information in as many diverse ways as possible.

A few guidelines for use

- Don't interrogate people. It's seldom necessary to ask even the majority of questions in any one category.

- Employ follow-up questions. The questions contained herein are "triggers" which may engender a response that demands further clarification.

- Trust is essential for candor. The other party will be most honest and responsive when trust is established (e.g., they believe you have their best interests in mind).

- Never be content with a single question, no matter how satisfying the answer appears to be. Some people will attempt to deceive you to save their ego, and others will inadvertently deceive you because they misunderstood the question. I recommend that you use at least three questions per category if the answers are consistent, and six or more if the answers appear to be inconsistent.

These questions are rational, objective, and most of all, based on common sense and simple discourse. Try not to be distracted or to digress yourself until the answer you're seeking in any given category is forthcoming. For example, it's dysfunctional to ask questions about objectives if you haven't asked the questions to satisfy you that you're talking to an economic buyer. Discipline is best.

Ironically, the longer you take to find the right answers, the more you accelerate the business.

Good selling and good luck!

—Alan Weiss, Ph.D.

My Personal and Customized Questions: Qualifying

I. Qualifying the Prospect

This is the process of determining whether the inquiry is appropriate for your business in terms of size, relevance, seriousness, and related factors. In other words, you don't want to pursue a lead which can't result in legitimate—and worthwhile—business.

Questions:

1. Why do you think we might be a good match?

2. Is there budget allocated for this project?

3. How important is this need (on a scale of 1–10)?

4. What is your timing to accomplish this?

5. Who, if anyone, is demanding that this be accomplished?

6. How soon are you willing to begin?

7. Have you made a commitment to proceed, or are you still analyzing?

8. What are your key decision criteria in choosing a resource?

9. Have you tried this before (will this be a continuing endeavor)?

10. Is your organization seeking formal proposals for this work?

Key Point: You want to determine whether the potential work is large enough for your involvement, relevant to your expertise, and near enough on the horizon to merit rapid responsiveness.

My Personal and Customized Questions: Finding the buyer

II. Finding the Economic Buyer

The economic buyer is the person who can write a check in return for your value contribution. He or she is the ONLY buyer to be concerned about. Contrary to a great deal of poor advice, the economic buyer is virtually *never* in human resources, training, meeting planning, or related support areas.

Questions:

11. Whose budget will support this initiative?

12. Who can immediately approve this project?

13. To whom will people look for support, approval, and credibility?

14. Who controls the resources required to make this happen?

15. Who has initiated this request?

16. Who will claim responsibility for the results?

17. Who will be seen as the main sponsor and/or champion?

18. Do you have to seek anyone else's approval?

19. Who will accept or reject proposals?

20. If you and I were to shake hands, could I begin tomorrow?

Key Point: The larger the organization, the more the number of economic buyers. They need not be the CEO or owner, but must be able to authorize and produce payment. Committees are never *economic buyers.*

My Personal and Customized Questions: Rebutting objections

III. Rebutting Objections

"Obstacles are those terrible things you see when you take your eyes off the goal," said philosopher Hannah Arendt. Objections are a sign of *interest*. Turn them around to your benefit. Once you demolish objections, there is no longer a reason not to proceed in a partnership.

Questions (in responding to an economic buyer's objections):

21. Why do you feel that way? (Get at the true cause.)

22. If we resolve this, can we then proceed? (Is this the sole objection?)

23. But isn't that exactly why you need me? (The reversal approach.)

24. What would satisfy you? (Make the buyer answer the objection.)

25. What can we do to overcome that? (Demonstrate joint accountability.)

26. Is this unique? (Is there precedent for overcoming it?)

27. What's the consequence? (Is it really serious or merely an annoyance?)

28. Isn't that low probability? (Worry about likelihoods, not the remote.)

29. Shall I address that in the proposal? (Let's focus on value.)

30. Why does it even matter in light of the results? (The ROI is the point.)

Key Points: Don't be on the defensive by trying to slay each objection with your sword, or you'll eventually fall on it. Embrace the buyer in the "solutions," and demonstrate that some objections are insignificant when compared with benefits (e.g., there will always be some unhappy employees in any change effort).

My Personal and Customized Questions: Establishing objectives

IV. Establishing Objectives

Objectives are the *outcomes* which represent the client's desired and improved conditions. They are never inputs (e.g., reports, focus groups, manuals) but rather always outputs (e.g., increased sales, reduced attrition, improved teamwork). Clear objectives prevent "scope creep" and enable a rational engagement and disengagement to take place, resulting in much greater consulting efficiency and profit margins. (Note that items IV, V, and VI—objectives, measures, and value—are the basis of conceptual agreement.)

Questions:

31. What is the ideal outcome you'd like to experience?

32. What results are you trying to accomplish?

33. What better product/service/customer condition are you seeking?

34. Why are you seeking to do this (work/project/engagement)?

35. How would the operation be different as a result of this work?

36. What would be the return on investment (sales, assets, equity, etc.)?

37. How would image/repute/credibility be improved?

38. What harm (e.g., stress, dysfunction, turf wars, etc.) would be alleviated?

39. How much would you gain on the competition as a result?

40. How would your value proposition be improved?

Key Points: Most buyers know what they want *but not necessarily what they* need. *By pushing the buyer on the end results you are helping to articulate and formalize the client's perceived benefits, thereby increasing your own value in the process. Without clear objectives you do not have a legitimate project.*

My Personal and Customized Questions: Establishing metrics

V. Establishing Metrics

"Metrics" are measures of progress toward the objectives, which enable you and the client to ascertain the rate and totality of success. They assign proper credit to you and your efforts, and also signify when the project is complete (objectives are met) and it is proper to disengage.

Questions:

41. How will you know we've accomplished your intent?

42. How, specifically, will the operation be different when we're done?

43. How will you measure this?

44. What indicators will you use to assess our progress?

45. Who or what will report on our results (against the objectives)?

46. Do you already have measures in place you intend to apply?

47. What is the rate of return (on sales, investment, etc.) that you seek?

48. How will we know the public, employees, and/or customers perceive it?

49. Each time we talk, what standard will tell us we're progressing?

50. How would you know it if you tripped over it?

Key Points: Measures can be subjective, so long as you and the client agree on who is doing the measuring and how. For example, the buyer's observation that he or she is called upon less to settle "turf" disputes and has fewer complaints from direct reports aimed at colleagues are valid measures for the objective of "improved teamwork."

My Personal and Customized Questions: Assessing value

VI. Assessing Value

Determining the value of the project for the client's organization is *the* most critical aspect of conceptual agreement and pre-proposal interaction. That's because when the buyer stipulates to significant value, the fee is placed in proper perspective (ROI) and is seldom an issue of contention. Conversations with the buyer should always focus on value and never on fee or price.

Questions:

51. What will these results mean for your organization?

52. How would you assess the actual return (ROI, ROA, ROS, ROE, etc.)?

53. What would be the extent of the improvement (or correction)?

54. How will these results impact the bottom line?

55. What are the *annualized* savings (first year might be deceptive)?

56. What is the intangible impact (e.g., on repute, safety, comfort, etc.)?

57. How would you, personally, be better off or better supported?

58. What is the scope of the impact (on customers, employees, vendors)?

59. How important is this compared to your overall responsibilities?

60. What if this fails?

Key Points: Subjective value (stress alleviated) can be every bit as important as more tangible results (higher sales). Never settle for "Don't worry, it's important." Find out how *important, because that will dictate the acceptable fee range.*

My Personal and Customized Questions: Determining budget

VII. Determining the Budget Range

Too much guessing takes place in the absence of a general understanding about how much the prospect intends to invest (prior to understanding the full value proposition). In many cases, the budget is fixed and entirely inappropriate, and in others it represents a better understanding of the ROI than that of the consultant! (Don't forget, this presupposes you're talking to an economic buyer.)

Questions:

61. Have you arrived at a budget or investment range for this project?

62. Are funds allocated, or must they be requested?

63. What is your expectation of investment required?

64. So we don't waste time, are there parameters to remain within?

65. Have you done this before, and at what investment level?

66. What are you able to authorize during this fiscal year?

67. Can I assume that a strong proposition will justify proper expenditure?

68. How much are you prepared to invest to gain these dramatic results?

69. For a dramatic return, will you consider a larger investment?

70. Let's be frank: What are you willing to spend?

Key Points: There is nothing wrong with exceeding the budget expectation if you muster a strong enough value proposition. But don't even proceed with a proposal if the prospect has a seriously misguided expectation of the investment need, or simply has an inadequate, fixed budget.

My Personal and Customized Questions: Preventing obstacles

VIII. Preventing Unforeseen Obstacles

As comedienne Gilda Radnor used to say, "It's always something." Inevitably, it seems, the best laid plains are undermined by objections, occurrences, and serendipity from left field. Fortunately, there are questions to establish some preventive actions against even the unforeseen.

Questions:

71. Is there anything we haven't discussed which could get in the way?

72. In the past, what has occurred to derail potential projects like this?

73. What haven't I asked you that I should have about the environment?

74. What do you estimate the probability is of our going forward?

75. Are you surprised by anything I've said or that we've agreed upon?

76. At this point, are you still going to make this decision yourself?

77. What, if anything, do you additionally need to hear from me?

78. Is anything likely to change in the organization in the near future?

79. Are you awaiting the results of any other initiatives or decisions?

80. If I get this proposal to you tomorrow, how soon will you decide?

Key Points: Make sure that your project isn't contingent upon other events transpiring (or not transpiring). If the buyer is holding out on you, these questions will make it more difficult to dissemble. Build into your proposal benefits to outweigh the effects of any external factors.

My Personal and Customized Questions: Increasing the size

IX. Increasing the Size of the Sale

Once conceptual agreement is gained, it makes sense to capitalize on the common ground and strive for the largest possible relationship. Most consultants don't obtain larger contracts *because they don't ask for or suggest them.* You can't possibly lose anything attempting to increase the business at this juncture.

Questions:

81. Would you be amenable to my providing a variety of options?

82. Is this the only place (division, department, geography) applicable?

83. Would it be wise to extend this through implementation and oversight?

84. Should we plan to also coach key individuals essential to the project?

85. Would you benefit from benchmarking against other firms?

86. Would you also like an idea of what a retainer might look like?

87. Are there others in your position with like needs I should see?

88. Do your subordinates possess the skills to support you appropriately?

89. Should we run focus groups/other sampling to test employee reactions?

90. Would you like me to test customer response at various stages?

Key Points: If you don't ask, you don't get. Don't throw everything including the kitchen sink into your proposal in an attempt to justify your fee. Instead, "unbundle" what you're capable of providing and add them back in at additional fee.

My Personal and Customized Questions: Closing

X. Going for the Close

Home stretch, but not across the finish line. Runners who slow up at the approaching tape lose to someone else with a better late "kick." Run through the tape at full speed by driving the conversation right through the close of the sale and the check clearing the bank.

Questions:

91. If the proposal reflects our last discussions, how soon can we begin?

92. Is it better to start immediately, or wait for the first of the month?

93. Is there anything at all preventing our working together at this point?

94. How rapidly are you prepared to begin once you see the proposal?

95. If you get the proposal tomorrow, can I call Friday at 10 for approval?

96. While I'm here, should I begin some of the preliminary work today?

97. Would you like to shake hands and get started, proposal to follow?

98. Do you prefer a corporate check or to wire the funds electronically?

99. May I allocate two days early next week to start my interviews?

100. Can we proceed?

Key Points: There is never *a better time than when you're in front of the buyer and he or she is in agreement and excited about the project. Even without a proposal, beginning immediately "pours cement" on the conceptual agreement and greatly diminishes the possibility of being derailed by surprise.*

My Personal and Customized Questions:

XI. The Most Vital Question

All of the preceding 100 questions are actually based on the reaction to one question which we often fail to ask of the most difficult person of all. And unlike most of the prior inquiries, it's a simple binary question, with a clear "yes or no" response.

Question:

101. Do you believe it yourself?

Key Points: The first sale is always to yourself.

My Personal Notes and Action List:

Alan Weiss, Ph.D.
President
Summit Consulting Group, Inc.
Box 1009
East Greenwich, RI 02818
Phone: 401/884-2778   Fax: 401/884-5068
Alan@summitconsulting.com
http://www.summitconsulting.com

Visit our web site for:

- Subscription to our free, monthly electronic newsletter: *Balancing Act: Blending Life, Work, and Relationships*

- Inclusion on our notification list for new products, workshops, and services

- Access to over 80 free, indexed articles

- Access to a variety of other resources for self-development and professional growth

- Application for inclusion in our Resource Catalog

Action Items

Sample Proposals

We've included sample proposals that sometimes adhere exactly to the system, sometimes partly use the system, and sometimes short-cut the system using only elements of it (letters of agreement, confirmations, etc.). However, all were based upon previously established conceptual agreement, and all provide a single fee for the project (or for each choice of yeses).

The normal framework for the value pricing proposal should encompass this basic sequence:

1. Situation Appraisal: Summarize and reconfirm the conceptual agreement concerning the condition to be improved and the desired state.

2. Objectives: The outcomes expected, both tangible and intangible, quantifiable and non-quantifiable. These should be expressed in terms of impact on the client's business—the improvement of the client's condition.

3. Metrics: How will the client evaluate success? What are the indicators that the objectives have been met? Simply stated: How would clients know that you both are making progress toward, and ultimately meet, the objectives?

4. Value: Either clearly stated or implied through buyer conversations, what is the value of achieving the objectives? This "worth" to the client helps to create appropriate project fees.

5. Methodologies and Options: What will be done to achieve the results? What "choice of yeses" are you offering?

6. Timing: Projects are finite. When do we begin, when do we end, and are there progress measures in between?

7. Accountabilities: What is the client expected to provide (documents, access, administrative support) and what do we provide (focus group facilitation, product, reports)? What is the nature of the collaboration?

8. Terms and Conditions: What is the fee (including the options) for the project, how is it to be paid and under what conditions? How are expenses to be reimbursed, and what is included and excluded?

9. Acceptance: The sign-off by the economic buyer.

The following samples don't rigidly adhere to this format, but all of the elements have been agreed upon either implicitly or explicitly. They range from the short-term and relatively low-priced, to the extended, relatively high-priced. Some are pure consulting interventions, other include deliverables. None is meant to be "perfect." Use them as templates to guide you in creating value-rich, high fee proposals for your clients.

Note that tasks are rarely specified in detail. The "what" and the outcome are important. The "how" and the input are up to the experts—the consultants. If the project is value-priced correctly, the margins will more than support unanticipated project needs.

Action Items

Sample Proposal #1

Major project dealing with large teams and functions:

Proposal to Assist in Reorganization at XXXXXX

Situation Summary

You must "jump start" people so that a new manner of working cross-functionally—in a matrix organization—is not merely accepted, but is exploited as a high-productivity way of life. Although reorganization has not been the norm, there is likely to be resistance, both from those inside and from those outside the new organization. A key factor—perhaps *the* key factor in success—is the ownership and appropriate behaviors of all key managers and exemplars, so that people have the proper leadership, and accountabilities will be accepted.

The primary transition is from a project-oriented transient approach, to a program-oriented permanent approach in managing the business. Standards, measurement, tracking, feedback loops, and ultimate ownership must be created and embraced. The *process* of ownership is central to success. Collaboration in a matrix structure with accountability thrust downward are important goals.

Objectives

Among the results to be achieved are these key objectives:

- Managers' skills are developed and behaviors are directed toward achieving and exploiting results that the new organization affords.
- Accountabilities are clear at the individual job (micro) level.
- Communications flow is rationalized so that people are able to deal within the "matrix" clearly, easily, and willingly.
- Key exemplars develop and exhibit collegiality that demonstrates support for and participation in the new organization.
- Group interactions are facilitated and continually honed.
- Obstacles presented by systems, procedures, and culture are identified and removed as appropriate.

Measures of Success

We'll know we're successful when the following are manifest:

- New programs are introduced in a synergistic fashion.
- Other XXXXXX functions accept and utilize the new structure.
- People are focused beyond merely getting something working toward getting it working to a degree previously designated which constitutes success. (It's not just running, it's running the way it should be running.)
- There is group approval, and a lack of cynicism; the programs show multiple sign-offs from diverse team members.
- Meetings and discussions clearly reveal that others were included—and valued—in the decision-making process, and that such inclusion was mandatory for success.

Value

The value to your organization in meeting these objectives includes:

- Focus is on the customer, not on internally perceived "threats," and consequent productivity loss.
- Senior level people can focus on strategic issues and not have to micro-manage.

Action Items

- Rumors are minimized as is their "default" position of "bad news" when people are uncertain.

- Rapid identification and removal of real obstacles.

You estimate that the total value of this project's success could mean well over one million dollars in reduced "failure work," saved productivity, and retention of good people.

Methodology/Interventions

The assistance in achieving the objectives would include, but not be limited to, the following activities:

- One-on-one assistance for all key managers in skills and behaviors required by the new organizational relationships.

- Group facilitation where needed in meetings and cross-functional teams.

- Group observation and feedback, with recommendations on how to improve the process.

- Assistance with written communications and meetings, so as to maximize ownership and accountabilities and minimize resistance.

- Recommendations for procedures, cultural norms (i.e., meeting types and durations) which will remove obstacles and strengthen the matrix structure.

- Assistance in creating ownership that encompasses standards, measures of success, monitoring means and feedback to those accountable.

- Observation and recommendations for interactions with "non-matrix" groups whose adherence to the new system is key to overall success.

- Attendance at large (off site) and small (on site) meetings to provide feedback on acceptance and recommendations on follow-up actions.

Timing

I'm available to begin working with you this month and, at the moment, the February 23 meeting date is one I can make. I'd suggest a 90-day initial phase, after which we'd evaluate progress in light of the above and make an assessment as to what further assistance is necessary. Our initial project would therefore begin now and last until April 15.

Joint Accountabilities

I would work with Cheryl (and anyone else designated) in conjunction with the project so that the interventions I'm involved in could be transferred entirely to internal people, if desired. We would jointly make determinations during the initial 90 days as to whether some of the objectives and interventions required more emphasis than others, and/or whether new needs arose that were unanticipated. In that case, we would redirect our efforts accordingly.

Terms and Conditions

My fees are always based upon the project, and never upon time units. That way you're encouraged to call upon me without worrying about a meter running, and I'm free to suggest additional areas of focus without concern about increasing your investment.

The fee for the assistance detailed above would be $15,000 per month, payable on the 15th of February, March, and April. If you choose to pay the entire amount at the outset, I'm happy to provide a 10% reduction in the total fee. Expenses are billed as actually accrued at the conclusion of each month, and are payable upon receipt of our statement.

At the end of the 90 days we would make a joint evaluation as to whether to continue the relationship and, if so, under what conditions.

Action Items

Acceptance

Your signature below indicates acceptance of this proposal and its terms.

This proposal is accepted and forms an agreement between XXXXXXXXXX (you) and Summit Consulting Group, Inc. (we/us/I) as represented by Alan Weiss.

For Summit Consulting Group, Inc.:   For XXXXXXXXXX:

_____   _____

Alan Weiss
President

Date: _____   Date:_____

Sample Proposal #2

Specific intervention to improve performance evaluation

Proposal: XXXXXXXXXX XXXXXXX—Performance Appraisal Skills Building

This constitutes a proposal tendered by Summit Consulting Group, Inc. to assist XXXXXXXXXX XXXXXXX, Inc. in the research, design, implementation and refinement of a performance evaluation process which is understood, supported, and effectively executed by designated members of management.

Objectives

The objectives for the project include:

- XXX management will possess the knowledge to execute performance reviews
- XXX management will possess the skills to execute those reviews
- Reviews will be conducted in conformance with company guidelines
- Reviews will provide useful and honest feedback to performers
- Performance improvement will be detailed and monitored

In achieving these objectives, the following parameters will be met in establishing and implementing the processes:

- alignment between individual and organizational goals
- linking tasks to output; that is, focusing on and measuring results
- seeking competitive advantage; the process must enhance business goals
- creation of a dialogue between performer and manager
- participation by and commitment from the performer and the manager
- simplicity of administration and avoidance of bureaucracy
- metrics for a *process* and not an *event*; follow-through and support
- combine skills and behaviors in the development focus
- global applicability, allowing for local cultural variations, as appropriate
- minimize disruption in implementation of and training for the process

Action Items

Measurement

The success in meeting the objectives would be measured by factors which include:

- Creation of developmental plans for all employees evaluated
- Improvement in performance measures during the year following the first review period[1]
- Evaluations are performed and submitted by deadlines
- Minimum of grievances/reviews requested over disagreements in evaluations
- Random sampling of population indicates acceptable frequencies of monthly and/or quarterly feedback sessions during the year
- Minimum returned and/or "overruled" evaluations by senior management

Methodology

Option 1: Skills Building for Managers

We would work with you to research and design a classroom intervention which could be delivered by our staff acting as facilitators and by your own people as internal instructors. This option would entail:

- Investigation of the types of jobs and performance currently required by XXX and those jobs and performance anticipated by XXX.
- Assessment of current managerial competence/success/failures in contemporary performance evaluation efforts.
- Incorporation of XXX business and strategic goals so that performance and assessment are aligned with organizational need.
- Creation of a one-day program, including concepts, exercises, XXX examples and support ("take-away") materials which would include:

  - how to coach and counsel

  - how to provide informal feedback on a regular basis

  - how to create performance objectives (behavioral and outcomes)

  - how to create measurement criteria

  - how to create developmental plans

  - how to engage the performer as "owner" of the process

- Creation of a "train-the-trainer" workshop of 2–3 days' duration, in which XXX people would be trained to conduct the one-day sessions.
- Creation of appropriate reference material and job aids for both sessions.
- Facilitation of sessions, as requested.
- Monitoring of results over ensuing six months and refinements as necessary as process is implemented.

Option 2: Skills Building for Remote Locations (Optional)

We would create a set of self-paced, objective-based (criterion-referenced instruction) materials to be provided in those cases when:

[1] Note that this need not be represented by increased *ratings*, since the goal is to improve relative to current performance, and forced distributions may still be applied.

Action Items

- Remote locations preclude classroom interventions.

- Small numbers of people preclude classroom intervention.

- Language difficulties require varying speed of learning.

- Refresher capability is required to update skills.

- New promotions or new hires cannot be accommodated in classes rapidly.

In this case, we would adapt the option 1 program into a set of print and video materials which contain their own criteria for successful completion, and can be validated by an off-site party, if desired. We estimate that this program would require from 16 to 24 hours to complete, and would be completely modularized. (We generally recommend half-day exposures.)

Option 3: Skills Building for All Employees in Performance Appraisal (Optional)

There is an opportunity to expose all employees (not just managers conducting reviews) to the need for two-party commitment to the process and ownership of it. By exposing performers to the basics covered in option 1, they are empowered to participate with a commensurate set of skills, and not be reliant on the reviewer and his or her prior training.

We recommend a three-hour session which fulfills the following:

- Employees are able to understand and question the process.

- Employees understand their accountabilities and role in the process.

- Exercises are provided in objective setting and measurement criteria.

- "Receiving feedback" skills are developed (people respond best when they know *how to be coached*).

These sessions can provide for an equal dialogue between manager and performer, and increase the frequency of feedback since the employee understands the need and his or her accountability in asking for feedback.

Option 4: Integration with the Performance System (Optional)

As a part of our research and design activities, we can "extend our reach" somewhat and recommend and design the best ways in which to integrate the performance evaluation process into areas such as:

- compensation and incentive rewards

- developmental plans, training programs, and career development

- identification of high potential people

- succession planning

- recruitment

- performance improvement/probation/remedial/termination needs

- culture and morale issues

Since the performance system seldom operates in isolated parts, but rather in a dynamic interaction, the improvement of the performance evaluation process can serve as a catalyst to enhance the other aspects of the performance system. This is a relatively straightforward undertaking when we are engaged in option 1 and asked to examine the interrelationships concurrently.

Timing

Option 1: Implementation by June 30

Option 2: Implementation by September 1

Action Items

Option 3: Implementation by June 1

Option 4: Implementation by September 1

Resource Commitments

Summit Consulting Group, Inc. will provide Alan Weiss, Ph.D. as the project leader. He will be continually involved in all aspects of the project, and serve as primary interface with XXX management. Summit's credentials have been provided in previous materials. We will sign nondisclosure agreements as requested, and all work in this project becomes the sole property of XXX. All of our work is conducted within strict bounds of confidentiality.

We will also provide all materials, audio/visual aids, computer work, and other support services as required. We will provide masters of the final, approved materials for ownership and reproduction by XXX.

XXX will provide us with reasonable access to key management people, documentation, and company information, as appropriate, within the time-frames outlined. XXX will be responsible for all scheduling of classes, facilities, equipment, and related support for training and development purposes. XXX will also adhere to the fee structure and reimbursement procedures outlined below. XXX professionals will assist in some data gathering, development of relevant examples, and critique of materials.

Note: Facilitation of programs will be billable at rates shown under "terms."

Terms and Conditions

We assess a single project fee for our work, so that there is never a "meter running," and you can control expenses tightly. Within the objectives and parameters described above, we will commit as much time as necessary to fulfill the objectives and meet the time frames. You and we may request additional time be spent on aspects of this project without any additional fees or charges, except for travel expenses.

Our fees for the options above are:

Option 1: Skills building for managers: $68,000

Option 2: Self-paced study for managers:

      print materials only 24,000

      print materials and video 46,000

Option 3: Skills building for employees: 12,000

Option 4: Integration into performance system: 18,000

Facilitation by our staff, any option: $3,500 per day, U.S., $5,000 non-U.S.

Training-the-trainer facilitation: included in the fee for option 1.

Payment terms:

  Full payment of $68,000 at acceptance in return for reduced fee structure.

Further payment alternatives:

  We will honor the fees for the optional methodologies through calendar 1995.

Reasonable travel and living expenses are submitted monthly as actually incurred, and payment is due upon presentation of our invoice. There are no charges for fax, phone, postage, duplication, etc.

This project is noncancelable, and agreed-upon payment terms are due as described. However, you may postpone or delay any part of the work in progress without penalty. In addition, our work is guaranteed. If we do not meet your objectives, and cannot meet them after your notification and an attempt to correct the shortcoming, we will refund your full fee. This has been our commitment to our clients for over a decade.

Action Items

Acceptance

This proposal is accepted and forms an agreement between XXXXXXXXXX XXXXXXX, Inc. (you/XXX) and Summit Consulting Group, Inc. (we/us).

For Summit Consulting Group, Inc.:

_____

Alan Weiss
President

Date: _____

For XXXXXXXXXXXXXXXX, Inc.:

_____

Date: _____

Sample Proposal #3

Letter of agreement confirming annual retainer basis

January 21

XXXXXXXX
President
XXXXXXXX
XXXXXXX
Pittsburgh, PA 15230

Dear XXXX:

I'm providing a summary of our discussion of January 19 which provided the basis for our working relationship for 1994. There are to be ten areas of involvement:

1. Monthly meetings between the two of us to discuss strategy, longer-term issues, and personal growth goals.

2. Personal development for each business head, based upon a series of ongoing meetings I plan with Tim, Frank, Bob, and Brian. These will be individualized and mutually agreed. In addition, I'll serve as a "sounding board" for them as they work to achieve their business goals. You will apprise them of this support.

3. Partnership with Jim XXXXXX, wherein I will assist him in contributing to the business as a senior manager and internal consultant, not merely as a human resource facilitator. This will focus globally, and will include improving the caliber of human resource professionals and hires. I have already established a preliminary discussion.

4. Responding to other key managers on an "as needed" basis. You (or the business heads) will apprise them of this support.

5. Work with Jim to set up and facilitate the next top-level review group, to assess value-added of people and positions.

6. Specifically work with the relevant managers to establish:

• a succession plan, and ensuing development plan

• a comprehensive educational plan for the organization

• clarity of field management's role, development, and key personnel

• sales analysis tools for effectively monitoring and managing business

7. Situational responsiveness to needs which arise and you deem require my assistance, which are not covered elsewhere.

8. Assistance in the preparation and delivery of the February sales meeting.

9. Working with the relevant managers to strengthen employee communications, particularly in areas of trust, credibility, and recognizing the importance of everyone's contribution.

Action Items

10. Quarterly meeting with Trevor to provide assistance as he sees fit, including suggestions for what he can be doing to enhance performance.

To accomplish these goals, I will increase my time allocation to XXXXXX by about 20%. Historically, we've both honored schedules very well, and some months might be close to 75% and others 10%, but the average will hold.

The total fee will be $100,000, of which $32,500 has already been paid. The remaining $67,500 will be paid in 10 equal installments of $6,750 from March through December. Expenses will be billed monthly, as they are now. I'll provide a monthly summary sheet of focus and results.

Let me know if I've missed anything. I've already received a call from Ron, and I'll be seeing him on some IS issues in February. I'll also be scheduling our time together with Fran in the next day or so.

It's a pleasure to have somewhere to go once again during such cold weather . . .

Sincerely,

Alan Weiss
President
AW/cca

Sample Proposal #4

Letter of agreement confirming specific focus group intervention

July 20

XXXXXXXXX
Executive Director, Sales
XXXXXXXXXX Division
Box 2000
XXXXXXXXXXX

Dear Carrol:

Thanks for your support and interest in this work. It will be a pleasure working with you and your colleagues. As promised, here is a summary and confirmation.

I will conduct 12 focus groups: two in St. Louis on August 7, two more in St. Louis on September 7, six in Woodbridge on September 21–23, and two in New Hampshire on September 19. I will also critique the survey you send me, provide mailers for it to be returned here, correlate and analyze the results according to the "cuts" you desire, and provide evaluation and recommendations as a result of the survey and focus groups. I will plan to send the report to you in writing late the week of October 3, meet with you to discuss it on October 11, and be available if needed for a presentation on October 19. During this period, I am available for consultation, fine-tuning, and discussions as you deem necessary.

Among other issues, we will focus on:

• hiring and retaining minority employees

• creating a diverse population

• promotion of diverse peoples

• turnover among female employees

• status and perceptions of employees age 40 and over

• work and family life issues

Action Items

The total fee for this project is $35,000, payable on or before September 1. Expenses will be billed monthly as actually incurred, and will include only reasonable travel and living expenses.

I will be arriving in St. Louis on August 7 at 11:04 on TWA 177 out of Boston. Please advise the dress code, since I like to dress as the participants do. Also, it would be fine to schedule the focus groups from 1–3 and 3–5, since they will actually run about 90 minutes.

I've always worked on a "handshake" with XXXXX and a single payment in return for lower fees. However, I'll be glad to sign any agreements you need. Also, please don't hesitate to call me at any time on our toll-free number: 800/766-7935. If I'm not here, I'll get back to you promptly.

Thanks again for your business. I'm happy to be involved with you on such an important project for XXXXX.

Sincerely,

Alan Weiss, Ph.D.
President
AW/cca
Enclosures

Acceptance

This proposal is accepted and forms an agreement between XXXXXXXXX (you) and Summit Consulting Group, Inc. (we/us/I) as represented by Alan Weiss.

For Summit Consulting Group, Inc.:   For XXXXXXXXXX:

_____   _____

Alan Weiss
President

Date: _____   Date:_____

(Originals to follow by Fedex.)

Sample Proposal #5

Very brief confirmation of small sampling project with existing client

April 8
XXXXXXXXXXX
Training and Development
WP53B-405
XXXXXXXXXXXX
XXXXXXXXXX
XXXXXXXXXX

Dear Burnette:

This is to confirm that I'll conduct six focus groups for you at XXXXXXXXXXX on June 14–16 to provide feedback for your diversity education plans. I will work with you and your colleagues prior to those dates to formulate questions, determine group composition, comment on your questionnaire, and help in whatever other ways I can.

The total fee is $18,000, plus actual travel expenses. The fee includes all of the preparatory work, the facilitation of the groups, analysis and feedback of the data, a written report, and a personal presentation of the findings. Travel expenses should be

Action Items

minimal. The fee is due on or before June 1. Expenses are due subsequent to the project, upon receipt of our statement. We will invoice the fee in a few weeks.

In view of the volume of work we've performed for XXXXX, this letter of agreement is sufficient for our purposes. Would you please have someone sign one copy and return it, and let me know at your convenience when you would like to begin the preparatory work. Thanks for your help. I'm looking forward to assisting in your diversity plans.

Sincerely,

Alan Weiss, Ph.D.
President
AW/cca
Enclosures

Acceptance

This letter of intent is accepted and forms an agreement between XXXXXXXXXXX (you) and Summit Consulting Group, Inc. (we/us/I) as represented by Alan Weiss.

For Summit Consulting Group, Inc.:   For XXXXXXXXXX:

_____   _____

Alan Weiss
President

Date: _____   Date:_____

Sample Proposal #6

Memorandum of understanding to conform to client's preferred format, covering major departmental restructuring

Date: April 15

To: XXXXXX
From: Alan Weiss
Subject: Proposal to Manage Transformation

Memorandum of Understanding

The purpose of this letter is to establish a clear understanding of the roles and responsibilities of the Order Fulfillment core consulting team and agreement on the outcomes of the consulting engagement.

Proposed Approach

We propose a three phase approach to meet the objectives of the Order Fulfillment program. Phase 1 has already started in accordance with our MOU of April 5 and will continue for 90 days. Phase 2 will take approximately six months. We estimate Phase 3 will require an additional 90 days. These phases are described as follows:

Action Items

1. Mobilization Phase

- Create the umbrella vision through facilitation with appropriate team participants.

- Resolve what issues can be "packaged" in common priorities, what conflicts exist, what opportunities present themselves, and what approaches are most tenable for resolution.

- Create an action plan for each issue—whether structural, cultural or interpersonal, including its priority, accountability for resolution, measure of successful resolution, and monitoring points. This will enable senior management to assess progress quickly and be assured that all key issues are being managed proactively.

- Assist in the preparation for, facilitation of, and evaluation of the May 17 worldwide XXXX meeting, so that participants contribute and derive ownership, leave with a common vision and expectation for the changes, and serve as role models for the district managers.

Additional outcomes or deliverables for this phase will include an accepted umbrella statement and vision, determination of how internal and external resources can be best allocated and coordinated and buy-in by key managers at the May meeting. Ongoing resolution of the priority issues identified will carry over into Phase 2.

2. Transition Phase

- The key priority in this phase will be the interventions, assessments, reinforcement and support for district managers to accept, embrace and support the vision over the ensuing several months. They will be the key leverage points for the successful transition to the new.

- This phase will also include the implementation of the remainder of the action plans identified in Phase 1; the identification and implementation of "re-skilling" required for the new organization; identification and initial resolution of employee, customer, vendor, supplier, cultural and systems issues which must be addressed; continuation of a comprehensive communications strategy based upon ongoing progress; and exploration of XXX and other linkages.

3. Follow-up Phase

Since we can be certain that "we don't know what we don't know" in such a comprehensive new effort, this phase will leverage successes and correct problems discovered in Phase 2, including education, rewards, systems and related factors. It is in this phase that we would provide for the effective transfer of skills derived over the course of the project to internal resources.

The Core Consulting Team

The Core Consulting Team will consist of XXXXXXXXX and three senior outside consultants: XXXXXXXXXXXX XX, Alan Weiss of Summit Consulting Group and XXXX XXXXX of XXXXXX Consultants.

Engagement Management

XXXXXXXXXX will be the engagement manager. With the core team members, she will set objectives, master plans, tasks, methodologies, responsibilities and measurements. Under her direction the core team will provide objective assessment of program status and propose guidance on linkages and leverage points. The core consultants will follow up tasks for achievement and work with the Order Fulfillment team members to keep the program in focus and on schedule.

Marilyn will recommend and obtain additional specialized resources (including internal XX) as needed to implement the Order Fulfillment program. As engagement manager, she will coordinate and synthesize work of these special resources for efficiency and cost purposes, and for quality of contribution. The core team will recommend and obtain methodologies needed to implement the Order Fulfillment program, and advise on alternative methodologies when appropriate. This will include visibility on practices outside of XX.

Action Items

Specific Responsibilities and Role of the Consulting Team

The consulting team will assist the Order Fulfillment Team in achieving its objectives over the term of the engagement. These include beginning the following activities in Phase 1 and completing them in Phase 2:

Preparation for May 17th Meeting

We will work with you to create an "Umbrella Strategy" to present to XXXX managers in which a common vision of the Ideal Order Fulfillment System is presented, showing the integration and coordination between the four component initiatives.

Coordination of the Four XXXX Initiatives

We will continue to provide assistance in coordinating the four XXXX reengineering initiatives, linking them to each other, to current programs and to short-term improvement projects as appropriate.

Facilitation

We will provide facilitation assistance to the Order Fulfillment team as needed, including developing agendas, processes and documentation to support the facilitation.

Governance & Coordination

We will validate and refine the governance structure to manage and implement the Order Fulfillment program. This will include coordinating and defining roles, responsibilities and protocols at the steering and operating committee levels as well as for the Order Fulfillment and consulting teams.

Sponsorship

We will develop a plan to create, secure, maintain, educate and measure sponsorship for the Order Fulfillment program at the Ideal, First, and Migration levels. This includes not only sponsorship by senior management, but by middle management throughout all of XXXX. Implementation of the plan will identify behavioral objectives and activities for sponsors to engage in as well as the involvement of Order Fulfillment and consulting team members. Throughout the engagement we will monitor effectiveness of the sponsorship plan and recommend additional measures as appropriate. We will also be available to personally counsel and guide senior executives and sponsors.

Risk & Opportunity Management

We will assess the risks which need to be managed, and develop a strategy for mitigating risk. This strategy will include not only the risk of failure to achieve expected outcomes, but the failure to capitalize on opportunities. During the development of strategy we will identify the factors impacting organizational effectiveness and change-related risks, including identifying those who will feel threatened by the changes. This process will involve one-on-one interviews with stakeholders and the employment of diagnostic tools. During the implementation of the strategy we will constantly monitor the environment, identify unanticipated threats and opportunities that develop as the project unfolds and recommend additional courses of action as necessary.

Transition/Change Management

We will define areas of change, identify leverage points, and assess readiness for change. We will identify key psychological, interpersonal, cultural and systemic change challenges and recommend interventions to meet them. We will determine how individual behaviors and attitudes have to change and what must be done with rewards and measurements to achieve these changes. This work will be through one-on-one interviews, focus groups and diagnostic tools. On the basis of our findings we will develop transition plans to build alignment where rewards and consequences are mutually reinforcing of the behaviors desired. We will identify re-skilling options for employees with attention to integrity, their self-esteem and the value system of XX. We will assist with the implementation, monitor progress and modify actions as needed. In some areas we may provide specific educational sessions on how to manage people in a transition to obtain desired behaviors.

Action Items

Communication

We will develop with you a communication strategy and plan that includes the means, media and measurements appropriate for success. The strategy will encompass both formal and informal communication avenues and provide a means of dialogue and feedback. It will focus both on internal and external audiences including customer segments. We will actively participate with the XX resources charged with implementing the plan and selling the changes the Order Fulfillment program will bring.

Products or Outcomes of the Engagement

The outcomes of these eight major activities are as follows:

- A credible umbrella story to present to XXXX managers
- Continuing development of a coordinated Order Fulfillment effort
- A governance structure that coordinates steering and operating committee resources and roles
- Active cascading sponsorship and field support that fosters and sustains changes in behavior
- Risks of failure minimized and opportunities maximized
- Controlled transition with positive behavior modification, conflict resolution, and minimal disruption to ongoing operations
- Rewards, measurements, and consequences aligned to jobs, skills, behaviors, and culture
- An active communication program that meaningfully involves people internally and externally to proactively build commitment
- Finally, an organic system documented to transfer these competencies to XX for managing future initiatives.

Fee

As quoted in our original letter of agreement, the fee for Phase 1 of this engagement is $55,000 a month. Expenses will be billed monthly as actually accrued.

We appreciate your interest in our consulting approach and look forward to working with you and your team to deliver a successful and coordinated solution for XXXX.

Sincerely,

Alan Weiss, Ph.D.
Summit Consulting Group, Inc.

Action Items

Sample Proposal #7

Typical proposal for major intervention and sampling, post-acquisition

Proposal for XXX

Maximizing Productivity Post-Acquisition

Situation Appraisal

You are culminating the largest acquisition you have ever made. You are concerned about productivity, performance, and profit, post-acquisition. The organizations, though more alike than different in most respects, nevertheless have differences in culture and approach that must be reconciled if the synergy of the combination is to be realized. In fact, all of the subtle differences might not be apparent, and it would help to determine and analyze what the distinctions are in daily operations, beliefs, and values. A large investment has been undertaken, and the natural results of such acquisitions are to reduce expenses through consolidation and staff reduction, and to maximize strengths.

You wish to avoid the anticipated and unanticipated problems and drains on productivity that often accompany such consolidations, and to keep employees focused on business goals to the maximum extent possible. Inherent in this process is sampling employee beliefs and opinions, and designing communications strategies that reinforce the corporate direction. Senior management is very responsive to supporting an internal change management initiative.

Objectives

The objectives for the project include:

- Determining the consensus of senior management around direction, corporate goals, and key values.

- Creating mechanisms for sampling employee beliefs, opinions, and focus.

- Creating communications strategies to align individual objectives with corporate objectives (reconciling objectives one and two).

- Creating employee ownership of the process (they are part of the solution, not the problem).

- Determining who the key sponsors and influencers are, and preparing them accordingly through feedback and coaching.

- Creating and implementing the change management strategy.

- Analyzing effects on and making appropriate changes in processes such as the reward system, performance evaluation system, recruiting and placement practices, communications channels, and structure.

Measures of Success

Among the business indicators that we have succeeded in meeting those objectives are:

- Maximum retention of customers, particularly top customers.

- Key external and internal relationships remain and are enhanced.

- Top talent is retained, and top talent can be attracted as needed.

- Productivity continues at a high rate.

- Performance standards are met and/or improved.

- Revenue and profit improvement are in place and sustainable.

Value

The value to the organization of attaining these objectives include:

- Shorter-term realization of the potential synergies of the acquisition.

- A sense of purpose, direction, and clear strategy manifest to employees.

Action Items

- Rapid determination of problems and unanticipated obstacles.

- Management repute is enhanced among customers and in the community.

- Models are created to accommodate ongoing and inevitable change.

- Internal resources are seen as leaders of the effort to maximize ownership.

- Minimum of management distraction on internal issues.

Methodology

I believe that the essential steps in this process to gather information, analyze the feedback, organize the change management strategy, and maintain vigilance over the effort would include the following steps:

Desired State

- Interviews with senior management to

    a) determine the values, beliefs, expectations, and performance that is required to support corporate strategy (future state)

    b) report back on any perceived differences in those areas (lack of consensus)

- Development, if required, of an "umbrella statement" that would position the post-acquisition organization's vision and mission.

Current State

- Sampling employees by focus group, interviews, and/or survey to determine their values, beliefs, expectations and performance (current state)

- Create ownership among all employees for the change process.

Analyze the Distance

- Create a plan to reconcile the desired state with the current state. This is the change management strategy.

- Determine who the key sponsors and influencers are, and educate and coach them accordingly in their roles as exemplars and leaders (close the loop with the senior people)

- Designate the behaviors and performance expected and how to measure.

Implementation

- Make the required changes, as needed, in culture, systems, and processes:

    - performance evaluation (for alignment with corporate objectives)

    - communications channels (for ongoing feedback and education)

    - recruitment and placement (for the desired state behaviors)

    - reward system (for support of corporate goals)

- Close the loop with senior management for ongoing sponsorship and exemplary behaviors.

There are three options in my experience that can effectively and rapidly address these issues.

Option One: Backstage Coach

I can work with you to set the strategy and planning for the various steps, which you would conduct and carry out using internal resources. I would serve as coach and adviser, on-call as you needed me. We would jointly establish the implementation plan, which you would carry out. We would begin with a planning meeting, and meet formally at least twice a

Action Items

month. We would confer several times a week (daily, if needed) by phone, fax, and e-mail. The benefit of this approach is that internal resources are seen as the sole implementers, it is a minimum investment, and it is subject solely to your time frames. It requires the internal competence, objectivity, and credibility to conduct and implement the steps. The disadvantages are that internal objectivity is never pure, employees are not always candid with internal people even when assured of anonymity, and the initiative can be relegated to the status of "another human resources program."

Option Two: Active Partner

Most of my work is as an active collaborator with clients. In this option we would jointly set strategy and plan the various steps, but I would be a key implementor in terms of interviews, data gathering, focus groups, and other interactions. I would be working with you weekly throughout the project at your various sites. (At the most, I would use two other resources for some interviewing, depending on the numbers involved. Generally, the fewer "filters" we use, the better, so I would attempt to minimize such use.) You would determine the extent to which internal resources would participate in interactive information gathering. The benefit of this approach is of using a professional skilled in these particular techniques, the advantages of third-party objectivity, creation and enforcement of time frames and deadlines, and the frame of reference that includes a varied range of Fortune 1000 organizations in similar situations. It requires mutual trust, the willingness to choose roles based on company need and not visibility, and total sharing of all information discovered. The disadvantages include a higher investment, additional coordination, and the discomfort that sometimes ensues from a "stranger" in the environment.

Option Three: Long-Term Audit

In addition to either of the above options, I can provide a "real-time" audit at intervals we agree on. After the initial project, I can return on a quarterly or semi-annual basis to develop additional samples, assess management reaction to performance, and analyze the extent to which the former "current state" has been abandoned and the desired "future state" is being embraced. We will then jointly design "fine-tuning" measures to augment the original plans and implementation. This is, no pun intended, analogous to a project "insurance policy." An additional phase in this option can be 360° feedback for key executives and sponsors to help sharpen their understanding of their impact and roles in the new organization.

Timing

I'm prepared to undertake this project virtually immediately upon your approval. As I mentioned, I take on only selected projects personally, and this one is of particular interest because I'm fascinated by culture change and its relation to performance. We will be able to very quickly make a difference in business outcomes, and your expectations for this work are business-focused and reasonable.

Barring unforeseen problems, I would anticipate completing all data gathering and analysis (executive interviews, employee sampling in all forms, etc.) in about 90 days; the analysis and change management strategy should require from two to four weeks collaboratively; and the implementation process should require another 90–120 days, depending on the scope we agree to tackle. These time frames apply to option one or two. Option three would begin three to six months after implementation is completed.

Joint Accountabilities

I will provide the backstage coaching or active collaboration support that you choose. As additional data-gathering resources are needed, I will provide veteran professionals from my staff in the New York (or local) area. I will provide you with progress reports in writing and/or in person as requested. My company carries full errors and omissions (malpractice) coverage. I will sign nondisclosure statements as you may require, and will agree not to undertake identical work with direct competitors without your prior approval for a period of one year after the completion of the project. I will meet our deadlines and schedules without exception. I will respond to all phone calls from you within 90 minutes, and all cor-

Action Items

respondence (written or electronic) within 24 hours. If we conduct surveys, we will provide the master document with postage-paid return mailers to our offices. We will provide the administrative support for all data-gathering compilation and analyses.

You will provide the logistics, administration, and scheduling support for data-gathering interviews, focus groups, and/or survey distribution. You agree to remit payment within the terms and conditions described below. You will inform us immediately of any changes that may affect the successful implementation and completion of this project. You will provide internal resources in support of the project as appropriate. You will provide us with access to key people, documents, and information as required to meet the project objectives.

Terms and Conditions

We charge a single fee for our project work. I don't believe that a "meter" should ever be running in such partnerships, and I don't want to place any client in the position of making an investment decision every time our help may be required. Consequently, you have unlimited access to me and our resources for a single project fee. In this manner, you know your investment from the outset.

Fee for option one: $65,000

Fee for option two: $110,000*

*(If you desire that I personally conduct all focus groups and interviews under option two and not utilize other staff members, I will do so. In consideration for that additional involvement, this fee will increase by 10%.)

Fee for option three: $15,000 each audit

                            $3,500 each 360° feedback

Payment schedule: A 50% deposit is required to begin the project. The remaining 50% is due 60 days after commencement. Option three audit sums are due in full at acceptance. Alternatively, we offer clients the option of a 10% reduction in fees if the entire fee is paid upon acceptance. (Option one would be $58,500 and option two would be $99,000 under this arrangement. You may also prepay for option three audits in this manner.) Once accepted, this project is non-cancelable, although you may request delays and rescheduling at any time without penalty. However, all payments are due in accordance with the fee schedule above.

Reasonable travel expenses are billed at the conclusion of each month as actually accrued, and are due upon receipt of our statement. Reasonable travel expenses include air, train, rental car, hotel, taxi, meals, and tips. We absorb all expenses for phone, fax, courier, duplicating, and administrative work.

Our work is guaranteed. If you do not believe we have met the mutually established objectives for this project, we will continue to work toward those goals with you for no additional fee or expense consideration. If, after such an additional attempt, you still believe we have not met your objectives for this project, we will refund your fees in total.

Acceptance

This proposal is accepted and forms an agreement between XXX (you) and Summit Consulting Group, Inc. (we/us/I) as represented by Alan Weiss.

For Summit Consulting Group, Inc.:   For XXXXXXXXXX:

_____   _____

Alan Weiss
President

Date: _____   Date:_____

Action Items

Sample Questions and Checklists

Proposals can and should do the following:

- Stipulate the outcomes of the project
- Describe how progress will be measured
- Establish accountabilities
- Set the intended start and stop dates
- Provide methodologies to be employed
- Explain options available to the client
- Convey the value of the project
- Detail the terms and conditions of payment of fees and reimbursements
- Serve as an ongoing template for the project
- Establish boundaries to avoid "scope creep"[2]
- Protect both consultant and client
- Offer reasonable guarantees and assurances

Proposals cannot and/or should not do the following:

- Sell the interventions being recommended
- Create the relationship
- Serve as a commodity against which other proposals are compared
- Provide the legitimacy and/or credentials of your firm and approaches
- Validate the proposed intervention
- Make a sale to a buyer you have not met
- Serve as a negotiating position
- Allow for unilateral changes during the project
- Protect one party at the expense of the other

[2] "Scope creep" is that phenomenon where a project oozes outside of its original boundaries, blob-like, because the client keeps asking for additional services and the consultant keeps providing them because there are no clear boundaries to the project. The result is insolvency for the consultant.

- Position approaches so vaguely as to be unmeasurable and unenforceable

Five Techniques to Master Prior to Creating a Proposal:

1. Determining who the economic buyer is and how to reach that person
2. Developing a relationship with the economic buyer
3. Establishing outcome-based business objectives
4. Establishing measures of success
5. Assessing value

Ten questions to determine the economic buyer:

- Whose budget will support this initiative?
- Whose operation is most affected by the outcomes?
- Who should set the specific objectives for this project?
- Who is the most important sponsor?
- Who has the most at stake in terms of investment and credibility?
- Who determined that you should be moving in this direction?
- Whose support is vital to success?
- Who will people look to in order to understand whether this is "real"?
- Whom do you turn to for approval on options?
- Who, at the end of the day, will make the final decision?

Examples of input vs. output (for objective setting):

Input	*Output*
• Run sales training sessions	• Improve sales closing rates

Action Items

- Conduct focus groups on morale
- Interview former customers
- Audit recruitment process
- Redesign performance evaluation
- Review expense procedures
- Improve senior officer teamwork
- Study technology needs of service
- Improve communication laterally
- Reduce attrition rate
- Increase retention of new hires
- Provide higher quality, more frequent performance feedback
- Decrease travel costs
- Enable decision making at proper levels
- Improve service response time personnel

Questions to ask to develop outcome-based business objectives:

- How would conditions improve as a result of this project?
- Ideally, what would you like to accomplish?
- What would be the difference in the organization if we were successful?
- How would the customer be better served?
- How would your boss recognize the improvement?
- How would employees notice the difference?
- What precise aspects are most troubling to you? (What keeps you up at night?)
- If you had to set priorities now, what three things must be accomplished?
- What is the impact you seek on return on investment/equity/sales/assets?
- What is the impact you seek on shareholder value?
- What is the market share/profitability/productivity improvement expected?
- How will you be evaluated in terms of the results of this project?

Questions to ask to establish measures of success:

- How will you know we've accomplished this objective?
- Who will be accountable for determining progress, and how will they do so?

- What information would we need from customers, and in what form?
- What information would we need from vendors, and in what form?
- What information would we need from employees, and in what form?
- How will your boss know we've accomplished this objective?
- How will the environment/culture/structure be improved?
- What will be the impact on ROI/ROE/ROA/ROS?
- How will we determine attrition/retention/morale improvement/safety?
- How frequently do we need to assess progress, and how?
- What is acceptable improvement, and ideal improvement?
- How would you be able to prove it to others?

Questions to establish value with the buyer:

- What if you did nothing? What would be the impact?
- What if this project failed?
- What does this mean to you, personally?
- What is the difference for the organization/customers/employees?
- How will this affect performance?
- How will this affect image/morale/safety/repute?
- What would be the effect on productivity/profitability/market share?
- What is this now costing you annually?
- What is the impact on ROI/ROA/ROE/ROS?

Questions to establish your personal contribution to value:

- Why me? Can any consultant do this, or do I have special attributes?
- Why now? Is the timing particularly urgent or sensitive?
- Why in this manner? Is there some aspect of the methodologies or relationships that are key at the moment?
- What's unique about our relationship? Does the buyer place special trust in me?

Action Items

- What's my unique value-added? To what extent can I "guarantee" success and exceed the buyer's expectations?

The nine components of a good proposal:

1. Situation appraisal
2. Objectives
3. Measures of success
4. Expression of value
5. Methodologies and options
6. Timing
7. Joint accountabilities
8. Terms and conditions
9. Acceptance

Joint accountabilities:

Typically included for the consultant:

- Hold details in confidence, sign nondisclosure agreement
- Agree not to work for direct competition without permission
- Specify which associates will conduct work
- Meet project deadlines
- Inform client immediately of unanticipated problems/resistance
- Keep client apprised of status
- Submit reports as agreed
- Carry appropriate insurance coverage

Typically included for the client:
- Meet payment terms as specified
- Provide access to people and information as agreed or requested
- Provide logistical support, meeting rooms, facilities, administration, etc.
- Agree to extend schedules if client cannot meet time frames
- Reimburse expenses as agreed
- Apprise consultant of internal changes affecting project

- Respond to inquiries, calls promptly
- Provide clear sponsorship and support where required

Ten golden rules for presenting a proposal:

1. Get it there fast.
2. Make sure it is error-free.
3. Ensure a faithful rendition of the conceptual agreement.
4. Keep it relatively brief.
5. Provide multiple copies.
6. Sign it in the acceptance segment.
7. Place it in a presentation folder or other appropriate package.
8. Enclose something of value (no, not a bribe).
9. Use hard copy, not e-mail or fax.
10. Provide a brief cover letter.
11. Specify the next step very clearly.

Ensure a faithful rendition of the conceptual agreement by using:

- As we discussed . . .
- Per your suggestion . . .
- In our meeting of the 14th . . .
- Your point about . . .
- Our prior agreement was that . . .
- We had stipulated that . . .
- We had agreed in prior correspondence that . . .
- As you recall . . .
- My understanding of our agreement is . . .
- You had specifically mentioned that . . .
- You specified that . . .
- My earlier summary, with which you agreed, said . . .
- Consistent with the reports that we reviewed . . .

Appropriate enclosures with the proposal might include:

- A book or article you've written that has been cited earlier.

Action Items

- A book or article by someone else that is relevant to the project.

- An example of findings or surveys from other firms.[3]

- A seminar or convention announcement of interest.

- An industry report.

- A software review or recommendation (but not the software itself).

- A personal or lifestyle idea (e.g., a vacation spot you've discussed).[4]

- Additional ideas for the project the client can implement alone.

- Information about a client goal (e.g., expansion in Europe).

To summarize, for a "command appearance":

1. Prepare yourself ahead of time with the buyer's input.

2. Take fees off the table and focus on value.

3. Use the resistors to help formulate the solution.

4. Close on the deal.

The causes for not gaining acceptance usually range among:

1. A legitimate, competing proposal was accepted

2. Your proposal was flawed in some way

3. Despite value, you were deemed as too expensive

4. The project was canceled or postponed

5. The prospect has decided to proceed using internal resources

6. You weren't dealing with the true buyer

7. There was an internal upheaval or reorganization

8. Someone talked the buyer out of using you (you were a threat)

9. Poor profitability has put a freeze on all expenditures

10. The situation unexpectedly improved or the problem disappeared

11. Unexpected profits have diminished the problem's priority

12. A scandal occurs in the company (harassment, embezzlement, etc.)

13. The organization is sold, merges, or divests

14. New technology eliminates the problem or opportunity

15. Some combination of the above

---

[3] Naturally, these would have to be nonproprietary and non-confidential.

[4] I once provided a chamber of commerce guide to the city where the buyer's daughter had just been accepted to college.

Action Items

Chapter Summaries
and Self-Assessment Questions

Summary of Chapter 1:

- Proposals are based on conceptual agreement of project outcomes.

- Only a true buyer can be party to the conceptual agreement for proposal acceptance.

- Timing is situational, based on how long it takes to move from initial contact, through relationship-building to conceptual agreement.

- Proposals don't "sell"; they confirm.

- Proposals are summations, not explorations.

- Successful proposals require diligent preparatory work.

- The prospect must be focused on value, not cost.

Self-Assessment Questions:

1. What percentage of the time do you submit proposals to clients prior to establishing clear conceptual agreement?

2. What percentage of your proposals are accepted?

3. What percentage of accepted proposals are unchanged by the client (especially the fee structure)?

4. How often do you focus on value rather than cost or task?

5. What do you do to ensure that you are meeting with the economic buyer?

Summary of Chapter 2:

- Only the economic buyer can truly accept a proposal. You should deal with gatekeepers through self-interest, guile, or force. Whatever you do, don't waste time at that level.

- Once you've ascertained that you've met the economic buyer and you've established a trusting relationship, there are merely three aspects of the project that require conceptual agreement *prior to your proposal:*

  1. What are the business outcomes desired (because that is the basis of the value to the client)?

  2. What are the metrics that will be applied (because those are the devices which verify that the value has been delivered)?

  3. What is the value of the outcomes (because that is how to base your options and fee structure)?

- Determine your unique value-added.

- There are specific questions to ask (cited above and again in the appendices) to complete any of these five "success" steps if you're not sure of the circumstances or what to do next.

- This preparatory work will be the main determinant of whether or not your proposal is accepted.

Self-Assessment Questions:

1. How often do you systematically verify that you're dealing with the economic buyer?

2. Do you have plans to successfully deal with gatekeepers in the short term?

3. Do you have the business vocabulary and contemporary knowledge to be seen as a credible partner for an economic buyer?

4. Can you recognize and/or create outcome-based business objectives for the potential project?

5. Do you ensure that you establish the value of the successful completion of the project in collaboration with the buyer?

Action Items

Summary of Chapter 3:

- There are nine components to a successful proposal.

- Situation appraisals are meant to briefly reestablish conceptual agreement.

- Objectives are the most critical element, and must be outcome-based.

- Measures of success can be objective or subjective, as long as you agree on the measurement device.

- A choice of options—of "yeses"—will significantly improve the probability of acceptance of any proposal.

- Acceptance should be immediately available to the buyer at the conclusion of the proposal.

Summary of Chapter 4:

- There are ten "Golden Rules" for presenting a proposal.

- Speed may not be everything, but it counts for a great deal.

- Submit a signed, completed proposal that can be used immediately to launch the project without further delay.

- Trust is the key to acceptance, not a legal contract covering every possible contingency.

- Content is crucial, but image is also important.

- Provide additional value with the proposal.

- Include a cover letter that confirms a follow-up.

Self-Assessment Questions:

1. What percentage of the time do your proposals include the nine components?

2. How consistent are you in developing outcome-based objectives, measures of success, and value of the project, the three most important aspects of the proposal?

3. How adept are you at establishing options for the buyer so that "How can I use this consultant?" replaces "Should I use this consultant?"

4. Can you provide a brief, clear, meaty proposal in less than four pages, successfully avoiding jargon and legalese?

5. To what extent is your proposal "buyer-friendly," enabling the buyer to immediate agree and sign off on the project?

Self-Assessment Questions:

1. How fast do you get the completed proposal to the buyer? Are you able to consistently provide it within 48 hours?

2. Are you proud of the appearance of your proposals in terms of image and professionalism?

3. How many "first hits" do you get, with proposals accepted upon submission without having to make additional changes or revisit the client to review the proposal?

4. Are you sending hard copy proposals, or are you relying on fax and e-mail? (Even if the client requests electronic media, there is no substitute for hard copy.)

5. How often do you send a personalized cover letter that formalizes a follow-up procedure?

Action Items

Summary of Chapter 5:

- Follow-up must be planned and confirmed in advance.

- Follow-up should be a continuation of the relationship, not a re-start.

- Never discuss fees; discuss value.

- There are non-responsive buyers who can't be changed. Don't go crazy.

- Learn from those situations in which you are unsuccessful.

- Try not to burn your bridges.

Self-Assessment Questions:

1. How often do you confirm a follow-up when submitting the proposal?

2. What percentage of your proposals are accepted without having to renegotiate or make another appearance?

3. What percentage of your proposals are accepted after making adjustments or additional appearances?

4. How often do you feel compelled to lower your fees to gain acceptance?

5. Have you ever been able to obtain business from a buyer who didn't accept a prior proposal?

Summary of Chapter 6:

- The client's lawyers may be nice people, but I've never known one who improved a consultant's proposal.

- Try to avoid or minimize the use of formal client contracts.

- If you must sign a client's contract, read the thing before doing so. The fine print might cause you severe indigestion when you least expect it.

- Use your relationship with the buyer to break bureaucratic impasses.

- RFPs are almost always a poor investment of your time. If you do choose to respond to them, stack the deck in your favor.

- There is nothing wrong with negotiating over a proposal, so long as it's about value and not about fees.

- There is nothing illegal or unethical about investigating additional business while implementing existing business. This is technically known as "intelligent marketing."

- Stay flexible. Don't dogmatically follow any single path. Not even if I've recommended it!

Self-Assessment Questions:

1. What percentage of the time do you conclude business with the buyer rather than with purchasing agents, lawyers, or other intermediaries?

2. Do you provide the proposal every time, or do you allow the client to provide a contract without resistance?

3. Have you ever reached agreement with a buyer only to have the project vetoed by a lower-level intermediary?

4. Do you actively seek additional business within existing clients by bringing to their attention other problems and opportunities you've discovered?

5. Are you willing to alter your approach to get business given the uniqueness of any given prospect?

Action Items

Suggested Resources

Gedge, Judy. *A Legal Road Map for Consultants* (Oasis Press, Grants Pass, OR, 1998). Specific advice on legal definitions and ramifications.

Holtz, Herman. *The Complete Guide to Consulting Contracts* (Upstart/Dearborn Press, Chicago, 1995). Examples of contracts consultants can use with clients.

Jacobs, Deborah. *Small Business Legal Smarts* (Bloomberg Press, 1998). The 125 most common legal issues for small firms.

Kennedy Information, Inc. *Fees, Utilization and Other Key Metrics* (Kennedy Information, Peterborough, NH 03458). Benchmark your business against this exclusive study (based on data from firms large and small) and fine-tune your approach to fees.

Kubr, Milan. *Management Consulting: A Guide to the Profession* (Information Labour Office, Geneva, Switzerland, 1996). Twenty-nine chapters cover the consulting process as well as specific services—encyclopedic work that first puts management consulting in perspective, then dissects the actual process of consulting into five steps.

McCann, Deiric. *Winning Business Proposals* (Oak Tree Press, Dublin, Ireland, 1995). A practical, step-by-step, common-sense approach to the proposal process . . . with a software application.

McQuown, Judith H. *Inc. Yourself: How to Profit by Setting Up Your Own Corporation* (10th edition, Career, 2003). Everything on Chapter C, Chapter S, LLCs, etc.

Weiss, Alan. *How to Maximize Fees in Professional Service Firms: A Handbook for Professionals* (Summit Consulting Group, East Greenwich, RI, 1994, 1997). Over two dozen techniques to raise the fee on any project.

Weiss, Alan. *Million Dollar Consulting: The Professional's Guide to Growing a Practice* (McGraw-Hill, New York, 1992, 1998). How to dramatically grow a consulting practice.

Weiss, Alan. *Value Based Fees* (Jossey-Bass/Pfeiffer, San Francisco, 2002). How to establish fees based on value and options.

May be ordered from Kennedy Information, 1 Phoenix Mill Lane, Fl. 3, Peterborough, NH 03458 USA. Tel: 800.531.0007 or 603.924.1006 • E-mail: bookstore@kennedyinfo.com • www.ConsultingCentral.com